HOW PLACE NAMES BEGAN

By the same author

HOW SURNAMES BEGAN
Lutterworth Press

PLACE NAMES OF THE ENGLISH-SPEAKING WORLD
Weidenfeld & Nicolson

HOW
PLACE NAMES
BEGAN

And How They Develop

C. M. MATTHEWS

With maps and endpapers by
Peter McClure

LUTTERWORTH PRESS
GUILDFORD AND LONDON

First published 1974

COPYRIGHT © 1974 BY C. M. MATTHEWS

ISBN 0 7188 2006 1

ACKNOWLEDGMENT

The author and the publishers would like to acknow-
ledge the help given by Messrs Weidenfeld and
Nicolson, publishers of the author's book *Place Names
of the English-Speaking World* in which the subject is
treated more fully and at greater length.

*Printed in Great Britain
by Ebenezer Baylis and Son Limited
The Trinity Press, Worcester, and London*

Contents

CONTENTS

Introduction

IT IS easy to take place names for granted and to think of them only as names. But they all began once as meaningful words, and that idea can rouse our curiosity. We want to know—not only what they mean, but what sort of people created them, how long ago, and in what circumstances. Such questions can't always be answered, but language experts have been working on this subject—especially in England—for many years, and as a result of their labours we do know how a great many place names began. We can also follow them through the centuries and see the changes that often happened to them later.

Because the historical background is all important to our subject, we begin with a chapter that summarizes the waves of invaders who peopled Britain long ago and between them gave most of the names that we still use. Without some understanding of the differences between Britons, Romans, English, Danes and Normans, one really can't appreciate British place names at all.

The next six chapters are devoted to the Anglo-Saxons (or early English), the principal name-givers of England. It may be asked why we don't start with the Britons or Romans who were both there before the English, but that is not as simple as it sounds. The pre-English names—which are numerous and important—exist today only because the English heard them and adapted them to their own way of speech, often adding English words to them. In the name of Canterbury, for instance, the first syllable comes from the ancient British name for that region, recorded by Greek sailors before the birth of Christ, but the rest of the name is typically English. In fact it is difficult to write of the earliest of our names without constant reference to the English. Therefore we start with their arrival in Britain and see something of their style of naming, before glancing back to the older names which they inherited. But the older names are not neglected. Chapters III and IV are much concerned with them.

In Chapters VIII and IX we look at the effects of the Danish and Norman invasions, and in Chapter X we skip rapidly through the centuries to the present day. This is a long span for one chapter, but space is limited, and as most of our best-known names date from before the Norman Conquest it seemed best to concentrate on the earlier period. But the making of place names is not all in the past. It still goes on today, and I hope that this book will encourage its readers to take an interest in the question of finding suitable names for new developments, and of preserving old ones where possible.

Next we try to make the picture more complete by taking a quick look at the place names of Wales, Scotland and Ireland. This is done largely for the benefit of the great majority who know no Celtic language. Those who know Welsh and Gaelic will not need so much explanation about the meanings of common words, but even they may learn something about their historic names.

After this rapid survey of the British Isles, Chapter XIV gathers together some outstanding points from the whole complicated picture, and shows how the mixture of languages has produced a rich variety of naming. This chapter also draws attention to some of the many pitfalls that beset the subject, and to the proper methods of finding true meanings where possible. It would be misleading to suggest that it is easy.

The first step towards the understanding of place names is to have some knowledge of the principal elements, or parts, of which they are formed. The common elements were all ordinary words once, and many of them—like "hill" and "ford"— still are. Others are obsolete and exist only in place names. The lists on pages 170–73 are designed to help you to recognize these. The elements are given as they normally appear in place names and not in their original Old English or Gaelic forms. (But the Welsh list consists of standard Welsh words because they have generally kept their correct forms in place names.) The page numbers tell you where to look for more information about each element, because the one or two words of explanation in the list are only brief indications.

One of the difficulties in writing of such a complicated subject is that the races who peopled Britain have been known by different names at different times. The Anglo-Saxons became the English, the Britons became the Welsh, and so forth. I have tried to keep this as clear as possible and the notes on languages on pages 168–9 are intended also to clarify the various races who spoke the languages. The word "Brittonic" is now coming into use by scholars to avoid the confusion between "British" as applied to the ancient Britons, and the much wider modern use of the same word.

As we turn to the broader subject of the overseas lands where British settlers (in the modern sense) have made their homes, we find the place names easier to understand because they were given in times so much nearer our own, and often the reasons for the choice are well recorded. But they too have the variety given by many languages, for wherever the British have settled they have taken over some of the names that were made by others who were there before them, and these names of alien origin are now ours by adoption.

For many reasons the place names of the younger countries are rather different in character from the older ones of Britain, but they are just as interesting in their own way. They too can tell us much about the people who made them, their hopes and adventures, their tastes and loyalties. They are part of the same story, a story that began in Britain and then branched out across the world.

Molly Matthews
Dorset, 1973

Invaders

WHENEVER PEOPLE of any sort, from ancient to modern times, come into a land that is new to them, a land where they mean to settle and make their homes, they begin at once to name their surroundings. This is something that cannot wait. They must talk at once of the rivers and hills they have seen, of the places where their animals can graze, and where they will make their camps, and as they speak names are born. They may not be thinking about names, probably not. They only say "the dark pool", or "the deep ford", or "the marsh", but their words will one day be formal names— Blackpool, Deptford, Slough.

If there were earlier inhabitants who have been conquered or driven out, the newcomers may have heard them speak of their land and have picked up some of their words, hardly understanding them, but finding them useful as ready-made names. In this way the Angles and Saxons, foraging across Britain from the fifth century A.D. onwards, heard many words—strange to them—which they adopted as place names: Avon (river), Crewe (stepping stones), Malvern (bare hill). We think of these as English names now, but they were part of the language of the Britons who had lived in this island from prehistoric times.

In the countries overseas where British people have settled in later centuries they have named many places in these two ways, either by describing them in their own words—Newfoundland, Blue Mountains—or by adopting the names used by the earlier inhabitants. Often too when the settlers have planned to build a city they have reproduced a name from England or chosen to honour a great man by using his name, as at Washington and Wellington. But this sort of thing was never done by the English in their own land, at least not before the Norman Conquest, and most of our place names are at least as old as that.

Place names in Britain arose from natural speech and each one tells us some special fact about the place as it was when invading tribes of remote times first saw it or talked of it. And the fact mentioned was the one that made the place important to them, whether as a good river-crossing or a strong defensive position, or simply as the spot chosen by their leader for his home. So to understand these names we must have in mind the invaders who peopled the land in the earliest part of our recorded history.

The first inhabitants of Britain whose language we know anything about were part of the great Celtic race who spread across Europe from about 500 B.C. They consisted of many tribes, ruled by many kings and by their priests, the Druids. They were a clever race, skilled in metalwork, loving poetry, brave and warlike, but they did not practise the art of writing and therefore in many ways they remain mysterious to us.

They had spread into Britain and lived there for several centuries before the Romans came to conquer them. They called it *Albion*, the oldest known name for this island. It has often been said that this name comes from the Latin *albus*, meaning white, but it was in use long before the Romans came here, even before they had become a great nation. Some scholars say it means simply "the land" in the Celtic language. The first account we have of Albion comes from the Greek explorer, Pytheas, who sailed right round it in the fourth century B.C. and recorded a few names from those wild coasts that seemed to be at the world's end. One was *Kantion*, now Kent, the first recorded name that is still in use in Britain.

When Julius Caesar commanded the Roman armies, he fought many campaigns against the Celtic tribes of Europe called the Gauls. Then in 55 B.C. he attacked their kinsmen across the Channel. They were known as the Britanni and he called their land *Britannia* after them. As he was the ruler of the civilized world, others followed his lead and from that time the old name, Albion, gradually lapsed.

Nearly a century later the Romans came to Britain again, this time to conquer and hold the land. For almost four hundred years Britain was part of their empire. But at last their power crumbled and in about the year A.D. 400 they withdrew their garrisons and left the Britons to themselves. They were now largely Christian and civilized and many of them must have known Latin, but their first language was still the same Celtic tongue that their ancestors had spoken before Caesar came, and their towns, rivers and hills were still named in Celtic words. Dover, for instance, means "the water" in their language. London is also a Celtic name. It means the place of Londinos (the bold one) but we can never know who he was. Both these names were in use when the Romans came.

No sooner had the Romans gone than a wave of barbarians swept in from the sea: Angles and Saxons, later to blend together as the English. The Britons, or those of them who survived, were driven into the west, and there they are still, for the Welsh and the Cornish are their descendants; and their language (which is called Brittonic in its ancient form) is still alive too as Welsh.

Some of the Britons, fleeing westwards, sought safety over the Channel, taking their name with them to Brittany, the second "land of the Britons". It would have been more reasonable for Wales to have had this name, for it was there that the greatest

number of Britons held their ground, but these
things were not decided on rational grounds; they
just happened from the way people spoke. The
invaders called the Britons *wealas*, which meant
"enemies" or "strangers" (hard that they should be
so called in their own land), and that is the origin
of the name Wales. The Britons, on the other hand,
began in this time of their distress to call themselves
the *Cymry*, or "brotherhood", and they called their
land *Cymru*, the name the Welsh still use for Wales.

Nowadays we use the word "British" for all the
inhabitants of Britain—English, Welsh or Scottish—
and very useful it is, but in the fifth and sixth
centuries A.D. when the Angles and Saxons were
sweeping over the land they and the Britons were
implacable enemies.

The Angles and Saxons never conquered the
whole island. There were Britons resisting in the
north as well as the west, and beyond them even
farther north were the Picts, a strange, fierce race
about whom little is known. And besides these were
the Scots, who came—strange as it may seem—from
Ireland. All of these merged together in the northern
kingdom that was called Scotland from about the
tenth century. We will hear more of them later.

The Angles and Saxons were closely related, with
much the same language and customs, and by the
time they had spread as far as they could over the
land they had become one people, though still sub-
divided under several kings. For a time it hung in
the balance which of them would give their name

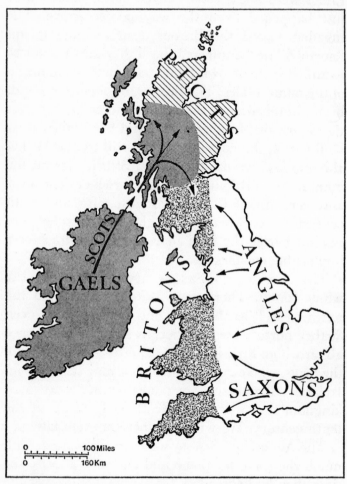

Map 1. Invaders and Settlers in Dark Age Britain

to the land they now held. It might easily have become "Saxony" or "Saxland", but the Angles just tipped the scales. No one made a formal decision about it; as with Wales, the name just happened, and while Angles and Saxons alike began calling themselves Anglish or English, their enemies still called them all Saxons. Today when a Scot or a Welshman calls an Englishman *Sassenach* or *Sasnaig* he is saying "Saxonish".

The word "Saxon" comes from the short sword, the *seax*, that the Britons knew only too well. "Angle" comes from Angeln in north Germany, the place from which most of the tribes set out: it is just where Denmark juts out and means literally the corner or angle.

The Saxons have left their name in many parts of the south of England. Essex, Sussex, and Middlesex were the lands of the East, South and Middle Saxons. The great King Alfred, who lived in the ninth century, was King of Wessex (the West Saxons) but he spoke of his people as the "Angle-kin", or English folk, and in his lifetime both Angles and Saxons began to call all their land England.

The English were never to lose the land they had won, but two more invasions swept over them with lasting effect. In the ninth century came the Danes, killing and destroying, as they themselves had once done. The Danes did not drive out the English but settled in among them, bringing new words to the language and new names to the land.

Lastly in 1066 came William of Normandy with his mailed knights. This was not a great invasion in numbers, but it gave England a King who held the land in a powerful grip. It changed the whole life of the English and even their speech, for many French words entered the language at that time. But one thing it did was to make England so strong that there has never been another successful invasion since.

Now the mixture was complete, and by the time the Normans had settled down and built their castles the land was almost fully named. Of course more names have been added since then. We often need names for new developments, but nearly always we use an old one that is already there. We build an airport and call it Gatwick because it was a "goat farm" about a thousand years ago and the name has remained ever since; or we call a new London borough Brent because the River Brent flows through it—and that name has been there two thousand years as you may read in Chapter 4. Every acre of Britain, every hill and stream and wood has a name, and most of them were given in that early period when Britons, Romans, English, Danes and Normans fought their way in.

2

The First English Settlements

OF ALL the invaders of Britain described in the last
chapter, those who made most of the place names
that we still use were the Anglo-Saxons or early
English; and we start our detailed look at place
names with them. We shall glance back sometimes at the older names that they picked up from
captured Britons, but these are best seen from the
English point of view. For the moment we think of
fierce Angles and Saxons seizing the land, driving
out the Britons, and making themselves at home.

Many of the Britons had been living in well-built
farms of Roman style, but the English barbarians
cared nothing for these. Indeed they seem positively
to have disliked the luxurious buildings with their
painted walls and mosaic floors, perhaps fearing

them to be haunted by the ghosts of their old inhabitants. Certain it is they preferred to make themselves new dwellings elsewhere in their own rough style, and the spots they chose—hundreds of them—and named in their own words are now our modern towns and villages.

They were expert woodmen. Their axes were slung by their sides and the first thing they did when a place had been chosen for a camp was to fell trees and put up a stockade to keep off wild beasts and enemies. Their word for this rough fence was *tun* (pronounced toon). The next thing was to build a shelter in which to sleep; and soon the word *tun* was being used for the whole encampment.

This word has played a bigger part in English place names than any other, for it is the *-ton* that ends thousands of them. Besides this it has remained alive in the language, changing its meaning as the early settlements grew into villages, and some of those villages grew bigger still, and it is now our familiar word "town". But in giving the meaning of a place name it would be wrong to modernise *-ton* as "town", for in the days when the name arose it meant nothing like that. Hilton was not a hill-town but a hill-farm, or perhaps only an enclosure.

In some place names we can see this earliest meaning clearly. Bolton, for instance, means a *tun* with a building or dwelling, and that would only make sense if there were others near by that had none. Barton was an enclosure for barley. Leighton was an enclosure for leeks; these grew wild, but the

English seem to have cultivated them from early times, and they used the word in a general way for all sorts of vegetables—so Leighton was the vegetable patch.

Soon there were so many *tuns* that each one needed some description to distinguish it from others. The home farm where the settlers lived first might be called the *ham tun* (now Hampton), and then when a second or third enclosure was made it might be the new *tun* (Newton) while the first became the old one (Alton). Others might be to the north (Norton) or south (Sutton), or in between them (Middleton). Weston is still easy to understand, but Easton has often developed into Aston which is not as obvious. There were endless ways of describing the different settlements: Ashton, a farm by an ash-tree; Thornton, among hawthorns; Upton, on higher ground; Netherton, lower down; Wootton, or Wotton, by a wood; Morton, on a moor; Marston, by a marsh; Poulton, by a pool; Dalton, in the dale; Grafton, by a grove of trees; Shepton (or Shipton), a sheep-farm, or only a sheep-fold.

You can see from these names that those early English settlers spoke much the same language as we do, but if we could hear them talk we should not understand. Too many sounds have changed. To them an oak was *ac*, a stone was *stan*. As our place names mostly keep the old sounds, we have places called Acton and Stanton, once farms by oaks and stones. The language spoken then is sometimes called Anglo-Saxon, but more correctly Old English.

Many Old English words are still full of life; others now seem old fashioned. We see them in old books and poetry but never use them in our speech except in place names. The old word for a lake was "mere" which makes the first part of our many Mertons and Martons; a valley was a "dene", as in Denton and Denham.

Many other words have gone completely. The old English word for a river was *ea* (pronounced ee-a), and each town or village called Eaton or Eton was once a river farm. The smooth, rounded end of a hill was a *hoh*. This word survives in Plymouth Hoe and Sutton Hoo, and also in places called Hutton or Houghton. The wild boar that lived in the forests was called *eofor*, and this word lives on in Everton, which was perhaps a place where the animals were penned inside a fence and kept as a herd of swine. Swinton has the same meaning, but Swindon means "swine hill".

Although *tun* was the commonest word for a settlement it was not by any means the only one. The common ending -*ham* is the old form of our word "home", and that is how hundreds of those Anglo-Saxons spoke of their farms. Their word *stede* meant just a place, but it too was often used for a farm or added to *ham* to make names like Hampstead and Hempstead, which in spite of their varied spellings are all really homesteads. Nuthampstead was a farm among nut-trees, Berkhamsted among birches.

24

Two more long-forgotten words for early dwelling-places are *worth* and *wic*. The first of these (which could also take the form of *worthy*) had just the same meaning as *tun*: first an enclosure and then a farm. Tamworth was a farm on the River Tame. Lutterworth means the clean farm (probably it had a good spring of pure water and the first part of the word referred to that). Woolfardisworthy, a long name for a small Devon village (pronounced Woolsery), was once the farm of a Saxon called Wulfhard.

Wic makes the endings -*wick* and -*wich*, which are often pronounced only as -ick and -ich. It seems to have been used for farms that had each a special use. Chiswick was the cheese *wic*, or dairy farm, and Keswick is the same thing expressed in northern speech. Several Butterwicks were known for their butter. Woolwich was where wool was dealt with, perhaps where shearing was done. Berwick was concerned with barley. Smethwick was where a smith, or perhaps several of them, worked with anvil and hammer. Warwick was the dwelling place at the weir, a part of the river that was dammed to make a pool to catch fish. Droitwich means the rich or princely *wic* and Nantwich the famous one—both of these were places where salt could readily be obtained; they were well known for this at an early date and the people who had settled there grew rich. In fact it is noticeable that a great many places with this name-ending grew into important market towns.

Although *-ton*, *-ham*, *-worth*, and *-wick* may all be translated "farm" or "village", there is a good deal more to them than that.

Some of the names mentioned in this chapter are such very simple descriptions in common words that the same names were bound to come into use in many different places. England has many Newtons and Altons, Nortons and Suttons and so forth. So in time it often became necessary to add still more information to a village name to distinguish one from another. Thus we have Kings Norton, which had become a royal manor, and Midsomer Norton, where a great fair was held at midsummer, Cold Norton, which caught the east wind, and Pudding Norton, where the soil was soggy as dough. The many Newtons include Newton Poppleford, which had a pebbly ford, Newton-on-the-Moor, and Newton Without, so described by the people of Wilton as being just outside their town. Anyone can find amusement collecting sets of double names.

Whenever a place name consists of two or more separate words we can be sure that some of them were added long after the original name was formed. Steeple Ashton, for instance: the ash tree from which the first encampment was named must have fallen and gone centuries before the steeple was built. The men who originally called it the ash *tun* were probably heathens who had no church and would not have known what a steeple was.

Our place names were not made all at once but

26

built up over the centuries. They carry echoes of different far-off times. But in most cases their oldest parts date from the coming of the English or even earlier.

Forts and Castles

WHEN THE English first came into England they
expected to have to fight hard to win the land and
hold it, and so they naturally thought much of
strong, defensive positions. Their word for such a
place was *burg*. This was not pronounced with a
hard "g" as we might say it now, but ended with a
soft guttural noise like the ending of the Scottish
"loch". This sound was later written as "gh" and
still remains in the spelling of many of our words,
such as "though" and "night", though it is no
longer pronounced, except occasionally as an "f"
sound, as in "rough".

This old English word *burg* still lives on in our
language as borough, the final sound having, in this
case, turned into a whole syllable, a sort of grunt. It
no longer means a fortress, but that is just what it

does in our place names. Because there were different dialects among the tribes of Angles and Saxons it exists in several different forms. Besides *borough* there is *burgh* (which is pronounced exactly the same) and *brough* (which is sometimes pronounced bruff). At the beginning of a name it is often only *Bur-*, and the common name Burton generally means a farm near a fort, while Burford was a river-crossing with a fort to guard it. But the most frequent form that this word has taken in place names is *-bury*, which although it seems so different, springs from exactly the same origin. Aldbury, Aldborough, and Aldeburgh all mean "the old fort".

The English applied this word to all kinds of fortified places great or small. At first they sometimes used it for the Roman-built towns that looked so strong with their massive walls but no longer had Roman guards. One of the first of these that they overran was Canterbury, which the Britons had called *Durovernon*, "the fort in the swamp". The English invaders paid no attention to that but called it in their own speech *Cantwaraburg*, "the fort of the men of Kent", and a few centuries of use reduced this to Canterbury.

However these Roman towns with their buildings of brick and stone were so unlike anything the English were used to that, as they pressed on, they felt the need for a special word for them and found it in one that they picked up from captured Britons. This was *castra*, a Latin word, meaning a military camp. When people borrow a word from another language they often do not use it with exactly the right meaning, and the English applied this one to any group of Roman buildings that they found and especially to towns. As with their own word *burg*, so *castra* came to be spoken in different ways by the various tribes, and it appears in several forms in our place names, but chiefly as the endings *-chester*, *-caster* and *-cester*.

Sometimes they called a Roman town by this name and nothing more. The famous city of Chester is an example of this; so are the places called Caistor and Castor. But more often if the invaders heard a place's old British name they kept that and added *-chester* to it. Thus Gloucester, which in the Brittonic language was *Gloui*, meaning "bright" or "shining", became *Glowcestre* to the English. By Shakespeare's day it was simplified to Gloster. Later still some scholars thought it had lost too many letters and put some back.

The English often added this ending to old names whose meaning they did not know and many are still unexplained. Manchester, for instance, was called *Mamucion* by the Britons. The English contracted this ancient name to a single syllable, and added *-chester*. They were even inclined to add it to London, which appears in ninth-century manuscripts as *Lundenceaster*. If that had stuck, our capital might now be Lunchester, but in this case the old name shook off the extra tag.

For a time *chester* was much used in common

speech, as we tell by the way it is combined with English words. Chesterfield was an open space beside a Roman town; Chesterford, a ford leading to another of them. When a swarm of Saxons invaded the south coast in 477 and captured the Roman city of *Regnum* they called it "Cissa's chester" (Cissa was one of the sons of their king). This is now Chichester.

The English picked up several Latin words besides *castra*, among them *strata*, which they used for a paved road such as the Romans made. This became part of many place names: Stratton, Stretton, and Streatham, for instance, were all homesteads built on Roman roads. Chester-le-Street means "the Roman town on the Roman road". *Strata* remains in our language as "street"; *vallum* and *portus* (two more Latin words) have remained as "wall", and "port", but *castra* faded away. It exists now only in place names, but in them plays an important part, for it helps—in its various forms—to name many of our most historic cities, and tells us that the Romans were there.

But the invading Angles and Saxons saw many other ancient strongholds besides those made by the Romans. Here and there all across the land the hill-tops were crowned with ramparts of earth piled up by earlier inhabitants, and for these hill-forts the English generally used their own word *burg*. In many cases the old defences are still visible as at Shaftesbury and Badbury in Dorset, Old Sodbury in the Cotswolds and Cadbury in Somerset, where perhaps King Arthur held his court. In each of these names the first part is probably a shortened name of some early tribal leader.

Of course the English also used this word for defences they built themselves. They named them in simple words, Newbury or Newborough (two forms of the same thing), Middlesbrough, the "middlemost" among several forts. Many bore the names of local leaders, but we know who hardly any of them were. One of whom we do know something was the warlike Queen Bebbe from whom Bamburgh takes its name. Her husband was King of Northumbria about the year 600. It was then called *Bebban burg*, or "Bebbe's fort"; this was gradually shortened to Banburgh and finally the "n" changed to "m". Bebbe must have been a notable lady for this important castle to be hers.

The Danes who came raiding the English coast in the ninth century had almost exactly the same word, and some of the *-boroughs* in the north-east were of their making. Scarborough, for instance, was the fort of a Viking called Skarthi.

Bury, Borough, Burgh and Brough all stand alone as place names in various parts of the country, but in most cases some further details have been added to make more distinctive names. In 1068 the town of Peterborough was entered in Domesday Book as *Burg* only. The monastery there had been sacked by the Danes in the previous century and rebuilt with strong, protective walls which made it a "borough" or stronghold. But other towns were spoken of in the same way, and so the local people began to add the name of St Peter, to whom their abbey church was dedicated, to make theirs different. The same sort of thing happened to a monastic town in Suffolk. It too was a fortified town, at first called only Bury, but when a Christian king of that region was murdered by the Danes and his body enshrined in the church it became Bury St Edmunds. Its own people still call it only Bury.

When the Normans conquered England they began at once to build strongly fortified towers which they called by their own word, castles. This word was new to the English but one they soon learned the hard way for they were forced to build the hated strongholds all over the land. Soon their own old word began to lose its warlike significance. It has not gone from our speech altogether, but instead of meaning a fortified town "borough" now means a town of special importance in local government.

The new word "castle" came rather late for making a basic part of many place names, though it is often added as a separate word, as at Burgh Castle where it repeats the same idea, "Castle Castle". At Newcastle it is a proper part of the name, one that needs no explanation. The castle there was new in 1080 when it was built by a son of William the Conqueror. That may seem a long time ago, but most of the *-boroughs* and *-burys* and all of the *-chesters* and *-casters* are very much older than that.

c

Rivers and their Banks

ALL THE early invaders of Britain came by boat,
forcing their way inland up inlets and rivers. And
whatever sort of contact they had with the people
who were there before them, the first questions they
asked were likely to be about water. We know this
because most of our oldest names are those of rivers.
The English learned them from the Britons, and
perhaps the Britons had learned some of them from
even earlier inhabitants.

Many of the oldest names have extremely simple
meanings. *Avon*, for instance, was just the Britons'
word for "river", and is still used in that sense in
Welsh. It may be that the captured Britons were
merely pointing out where the river flowed and not
saying its proper name at all when the English
first heard the word and adopted it for their own

use. Something like this must often have happened for there are eight Avons in Britain. Almost as common, though more varied in its form, is another ancient word for water which the Romans, who heard it from the Britons, wrote as *Isca*. The rivers they called by that name are now the Esk, the Exe, and the Axe. Ouse is another Celtic name, perhaps related to these, which seems also to mean only "water".

When Julius Caesar came to Britain in 55 B.C. the Thames already had its name. He wrote it *Tamesis*. (It was more than a thousand years later that the unwanted "h" was pushed in.) It means "dark" and so also do the river names the Tame, Teme, and Tamar, all coming from the same origin. Wye means "winding", and Wey is the same; Trent, "wandering" or "flooding"; Stour (probably) "strong". Darwen, Derwent, Darent and Dart all come from a Celtic word meaning "oak trees", and tell of the forests through which these rivers flowed.

The Britons of that pre-Christian time believed in a magical world of gods and goddesses who lived among ancient trees or in lakes and rivers. We hear echoes of these old beliefs in the story of Arthur's sword being thrown into a lake at his death and a hand coming out to catch it. Other echoes live on in our river-names. The Dee, for instance, was known in Roman times as the *Deva*, which meant "goddess" or "divine one"; and the name of the Brent, which flows through part of London, is a

35

shortened form of *Brigantia*, the "high one", a Celtic goddess who was widely worshipped.

But probably more ancient still are the river names for which no meaning is known. Among these, Humber, Severn, Tyne, Test, Colne and many others are names which seem not to belong to any known language. For thousands of years before the Britons came here these islands had other inhabitants, prehistoric men who built barrows and stone circles. If any words of theirs have passed down to us, they would be among the unexplained river names.

But although the English took over most of the old river names, they did name a few themselves, such as the Blackwater and the Blyth (the merry river). Waveney means "wavy river", and Mersey is the "frontier river" (there were enemies on the other side). The *-ey* at the end of the last two names comes from the Old English *ea*, a river.

They also had their own names for the hundreds of little brooks and streams beside which they made their homes. The words they used chiefly have come down to us as "brook" and "bourne" (or "burn" which is the same word) and any village name that ends with one of these tells of the vital water-supply which made the settlers choose that spot. Another common ending that implies a stream is *-well*, for to them a well was not the neat man-made affair that we think of now but a natural spring bubbling up as the beginning of a brook.

Sherborne means the bright stream; Blackburn, the dark one; Woburn, crooked stream; Redbourn, reedy stream; Lambourne, the stream where the lambs were washed; Honeybourne, where honeycomb was found on the banks; and so on. Prittlewell was a prattling spring, Ludwell a loud one.

All through our history, as far back as we can go, river names have helped to name much more than rivers; they have been used for whole towns and districts. The Romans, like everyone else, built most of their towns on rivers, and they called them by the river names they found there. The English often carried on the same name, pronounced in their own style, with the addition of -*chester* in one of its forms (see page 30). Thus Doncaster is on the Don, Colchester on the Colne, Lancaster on the Lune, Cirencester on the Churn (all sorts of peculiar pronunciations have happened here); Grantchester is on the Granta; Towcester is on the Tove, Exeter on the Exe, Alcester on the Alne and so on. Each means a Roman town on a special river.

There can hardly be a river of any size in England without namesakes. From the gentle little Wylye in the south we have Wilton; and from that came "Wiltonshire", now Wiltshire. From the River Dart in Devon we get the name Dartmoor, where the river rises, and Dartmouth where it reaches the sea, as well as Dartington, the farm of the "Dartings"— the people of the Dart. Trentham was a homestead on the Trent; Taunton is on the Tone, Plymouth at the mouth of the Plym; and so we might go on and on.

Even in modern times when we need a place

37

name—something that happens seldom as we have so many old ones—we turn naturally to rivers to supply them; and now names like Merseyside, Tyneside, Humberside and Avon are coming into use for new counties and county boroughs. So these ancient river names, some of them prehistoric, are taking on new duties.

Apart from actual river names there is much evidence in our place names of the way rivers were used. The English invaders came upstream in their long boats and seized the best-looking places on the banks. Here they kept their boats; and for centuries there was much coming and going and bringing of goods by water. The usual English word for a landing-place was *hithe*. Although there is a town called Hythe on the south coast, most of the places with *hithe* in their names were on rivers.

We see them all along the Thames. Greenhithe explains itself; Rotherhithe was for landing or shipping cattle. Lambeth was the hithe where lambs were shipped across the river. In some of the other place names the word has dwindled to nothing more than a vowel sound—but the old records show that Chelsea was a "chalk" hithe, while Stepney and Putney were the hithes of Stybba and Putta, who are only names to us now but must have been handy seamen in their day. Further upstream was the "maidens' hithe" though why maidens came there is not known. For some inexplicable reason, perhaps a joke, this name has turned into Maidenhead. Not far from there someone rigged up a windlass on the bank (this was a sort of gadget for hauling up boats) and the "windlass-bank" as it was called (*Windlesora* in 1050) has become famous as Windsor.

Dragging up boats was a common activity and a smooth slipway was useful. Ruislip was a "slip" among rushes. Often the boats were pulled a long way overland to some other stream; there they would be launched again. The name Drayton, found in many places, means a farm beside a "drag" where a boat or sledge was regularly pulled, and Draycott was a single hut in such a place.

From a different point of view, that of travellers on foot or horseback, rivers were barriers to be crossed. Few bridges were left from the Roman occupation, and from the start of their invasion the English were always looking for the best natural fords. Once found, these fords were remembered for future use; soon tracks led to them; and then they became meeting places, trading places, and places to be held against enemies. That is why *-ford* is not only one of our commonest endings, but ends the names of many of our old historic towns. Here are a few of them that grew important in early times: Hereford, the army ford, a strategic place to cross the Wye; Hertford, where harts (or stags) were seen; Stafford, with a *staeth* or special sort of landing place; Stamford (the same as Stanford), a stony ford; Stratford—several of them—where a Roman road crossed a river; Chingford, a shingly ford; Bradford, a broad one; Romford, a wide or roomy one; Oxford, where oxen were driven across;

Bedford, belonging to a local chief called Beda.

Of course bridges were eventually built in all these places, but by that time the names were so firmly fixed that no one would think of changing them. For that reason there are far more fords than bridges in our place names. But a few bridge names must be mentioned. At Cambridge a Roman bridge evidently remained intact; but the river it crossed was at that time called the Granta and when the English came there they called the place Granta-bridge. But after the coming of the Normans, who built a castle there, it became Cantabridge—apparently a case of people mispronouncing names in an unfamiliar language. For a time it was very variable until it settled down as Cambridge. After that people began to call the river the Cam. The odd thing is that *Cam* is a regular Celtic river name, meaning "crooked" or "winding", which is found in various parts of Britain. It could be that there was always a stream called Cam that flowed into the Granta and helped to cause the confusion.

Bristol was originally the "bridge-stow", the meeting-place at the bridge. It is first mentioned in 1063. Bridgewater is not, as you might think, the bridge over the water, but the bridge of a man called Walter who built it; he was Walter of Douai, a Norman baron. The Normans were great builders of bridges as well as castles.

5

Farming and the Land

ENGLISH PLACE NAMES are full of descriptions of the land as the Anglo-Saxons saw it over a thousand years ago. It was largely covered with forests, the valleys full of bogs and pools, the bare uplands rough and stony. Here and there ruined Roman towns and British farms made small patches of decaying civilization, but most of the land was wild.

The newcomers were skilled woodsmen and hunters, feeling as much at home in forests as we do in towns. They knew the different kinds of trees and plants and wild creatures better than most of us do, and hundreds of the places where they settled are named from them. And just as we have many words for different kinds of buildings, so they had a great choice for all kinds of woodland.

They used the word "wood" as we do, but also

spoke of "wald" or "wold" for woods on high
ground, as at Southwold; many of their wolds, however, have since become bare. Waltham means a
homestead in a wood. Then there was "holt" for a
big dense thicket, as at Northolt, and "shaw" for a
small one as at Birkenshaw (the little birchwood).
A very small wood or clump of trees was a "grove",
which is often -*grave* in place names. Gravesend,
which sounds so gloomy, was "the end of the grove".
A small wooded hill was a "hurst". At Hawkhurst
the hawks flew; Lamberhurst served as a pasture
for sheep; Lyndhurst was among lime trees.

An Old English word for a wood for which there
is no modern version was *bearu*. This has generally
become Barrow (but in some place names *barrow*
has a different source). Another was *frith*, which we
see combined with French to form the place name
Chapel-en-le-Frith.

But what those early English settlers wanted most
was land for farming, open land without trees.
When they found it they called it *feld* which we now
spell "field", but it was not at all like the neatly
fenced fields we know. Bramfield and Bromfield
were both overgrown with broom; Hatfield was
covered with heath (heather); they needed centuries
of work to make them into fields by our standards.

In many districts there was little of this bare
country and the settlers had to make do with open
glades in the forests which they could enlarge by
felling trees. Their word for such a place was *leah*,
which was later written "lea", and came to mean a

stretch of grass for pasture, because that is what the leas became in time. In place names, where this word plays an enormous part, it makes the common endings *-ley* and *-leigh*, and these take us back to that pioneering age when the woodman's axe was busy in the forest, clearing a space for his home.

Hundreds of village names end in *-ley* and where they are thickest we know that the forests were greatest. Sometimes the word stands alone as Leigh, but never seems to make the first half of a name. (Leighton has another origin, mentioned on page 23.) Generally it follows some description of the clearing and these vary endlessly. Perhaps the trees were mentioned: Oakley, Ashley, Thornley (haw-thorns), Berkeley (birches), Uley (yews), Boxley and Bexley (both from box trees), Notley and Nutley (hazelnuts), Bromley and Bramley (broom), Purley and Parley (pear trees), Plumley (plums) and so on. The wild pears and plums were small and sour.

Or perhaps the wild creatures seen there were the chief point of interest: Hartley, Hindley and Buckley (different kinds of deer), Harley (hares), Woolley (wolves), Borley (boars), Wormley (snakes), Crawley (crows), Finchley (little birds). When the settlers began to pasture their own animals in the clearings they used those names too. Cows grazed at Cowley, calves at Calverley, a stud of horses at Studley, and sheep both at Shepley and Shipley.

If it was a good-sized clearing it might be called

43

Langley or Bradley (long or broad). Filey was a place of five leas, which must have been small and close together. Shirley means a bright lea, open to the sun. Ugley in Essex was never what it sounds like; it was Ugga's clearing, and he was perhaps the first man to live there.

You would think that Beverley was one of these clearings, but in its first appearance—in a document of about the year 1000—it is spelt *Beferlic*. The first part is "beaver" (there were indeed beavers in England then) but the last syllable is one of the many old words for a stream. The same word makes the place name Leake.

Our names give many more glimpses of wild creatures that are now extinct in Britain, such as the wolf and the boar. The crane, a large water-bird like an outsize heron, was much hunted for food. It is gone now, but the many places where its name lives on—Cranleigh, Cranford, Cranfield, Cranborne, Cranmere and others—tell us how much it was once valued.

Another feature of the land, besides woods and water and open spaces, that meant much to the English settlers was its rise and fall. They liked to make their homes in sheltered valleys, if not too marshy, and preferred level land for ploughing, but there were many hills, and these too had advantages in giving shelter or for defence. In short the shape of the land was all-important.

They spoke of "hills" as we do still, but also used another word, *dun*, which we know better as

44

"down". This seems like a contradiction. Why call a high place "down" when it is clearly "up"? The answer is that the older meaning of "down" was "a high place", and when you descend to a lower one you come "a-down", off the hill, and so the second meaning grew. *Dun* in its high sense makes the common ending *-down* and the even more frequent *-don*. It was used for hills of every size, from a slight rise that we can hardly see now to a range of hills like the South Downs—or even Snowdon, the snow hill (which is of course what the English call it, and not its own Welsh name).

Huntingdon was the huntsman's hill. It must have been a small one, but even a little hump would give a view in that flat country. Hendon means "high hill", not very high perhaps but the highest thereabouts. Maldon means a hill with a cross on it. The cross must have been put there after the East Saxons became Christian in the seventh century.

By the time the English had penetrated to the west, where hills are higher, they were mingling rather more with the Britons and picking up more of their words, though often with little understanding. One of many Welsh words for a hill is *bre* and in one place where the English heard this they added their own word *dun* to it, making Bredon. Another Welsh word with the same meaning is *cruc* and the village names Crick, Crich and Creech, show the various ways in which the English pronounced this word. Evercreech means "wild-boar hill". Crichel consists of *cruc* and *hill*, just the same

45

repetition as Bredon, while Crichel Down means "hill hill hill".

As the English spread over the land they saw many traces of the people who had been there before them, particularly the burial mounds, of which many still remain today. We call them barrows and this word comes from the Old English *beorg* which was used for small hills. This has made -*barrow* and -*berrow* in some places, but it has been much confused with two other words, both mentioned earlier, *bearu*, a wood, and *burg*, a fort; and they can only be sorted out by a study of the early records. Farnborough, for instance, is not a fort as one might suppose, but a ferny hill.

A more easily recognized word for a mound or barrow has given us the ending -*low*. Harlow is the "army mound" and may have been the burial place of men fallen in a battle. Drakelow means the "dragon's mound" and must have had a legend connected with it. Twemlow means "between two mounds".

From hills we turn to valleys—but we will not find "valley" in our older names for it is of French origin, brought in by the Normans. The Old English word for a valley was *denu*, which names many villages called Dean or Deane, and provides the endings -*dene* and -*den*. Haslingden was a valley full of hazels. Harpenden was the harp valley, but why it was called that we don't know—perhaps the valley seemed harp-shaped, or perhaps a harper played there.

Among many Old English words for hollows, nooks and corners was a little word, *hop*, for a very small sheltered valley. This is the origin of Hope and Hopton and the endings *-hope* and *-op*. Wallop in Hampshire (which has now split into three villages, Over, Middle and Nether Wallop, and often raises a laugh) was once a well-*hop*, a little valley with a well or spring. Stanhope was stony, and Glossop belonged to a man called Glot.

Just as the English had no word of their own for a high mountain (nothing higher than "down" or "hill" until the Normans brought them "mountain") so they had no word for a deep, narrow valley. But at an early stage they picked up the Brittonic *cumb* (Welsh, *cwm*) and used it freely. This is responsible for the many villages called Combe and Coombe, and for about forty Comptons, all valley farms; it also makes a frequent place name ending, especially in Devon. Widecombe, for instance, was a valley full of withies, a kind of willow.

The English language has grown greatly and adopted hundreds of words since the time of the Anglo-Saxons, but for the things that really interested them, woods, waters, hills and valleys, they had a wide choice of words, including many that we have lost.

Men and Women

BEFORE GOING further we must give some thought to those men and women who made their homes in England from the fifth century onwards, building the *-tons* and *-burys,* clearing the *-leys* and *-fields,* finding the best *-fords* and generally making the land their own. Their own names are all around us.

They are, for the most part, strange and uncouth names that we would not recognize as personal names at all if we did not have old records to show just what they were; and their having been worn down by long use in place names makes them even more obscure. Here then are a few of the early adventurers who took and held land in the places where their names still exist: Aegil of Aylesbury, Gegn of Gainsborough, Sceaft of Shaftesbury (all commanders of forts); Gigel of Giggleswick; Gip of Ipswich (*Gipes wic* in 993); Glot of Glossop; Ugga of Ugley; Dudda of Dudley; Babba of Babbacombe; and so on.

Odd names, you may think, but fashions change in names as in other things. It must also be remembered that at this remote time surnames were not in use; people had only one name each and that gave the need for a huge variety and the constant coining of new names. Then again place names arose from casual talk, in which personal names were often shortened by familiar companions. Babba and Dudda sound like nicknames that have lasted from childhood, and there are many of that sort. (The commonest ending for men's names was -*a*.)

Another thing to keep in mind is that the time between the first coming of the English and the Norman Conquest—that is, the whole Anglo-Saxon period—was extremely long, six hundred years. During that time the people changed completely from the savage, heathen tribes who drove out the Britons to a well-organised Christian nation living as peacefully as they could until the Danes attacked them. And as they grew more civilized the kinds of names they gave their children changed too. In the late Saxon period they liked to make names consisting of two words of good meaning put together. Some of these we still know very well—Os-wald (divine rule), Eg-bert (sword bright), Alf-red (elf wisdom), Ed-ward (wealth guardian). These are just a few that have been remembered because they

D

belonged to famous kings, but there were a great number of different ones.

One of the things that shows the great age of our place names is that the personal names that are found in them are mostly of the early unfamiliar kind.

Look back now to those first invaders as they came ashore. They came in boat-loads, each with its leader, and each group was probably known by the leader's name. Sometimes a fleet of ships brought a large tribe which could seize a whole district, but these again soon broke into smaller parties. The regular sign in our place names of one of these tribal groups, great or small, is the syllable *-ing*. Reading means Reada's people (and his name meant the Red); Hastings means Hasta's folk, (and we know it was a large tribe as a wide district was called by this name for a long time). Beric's people settled at Barking; Muca's at Mucking; Snear's party at Snoring, which is now split into Great and Little Snoring (*snear* meant swift, so it was a perfectly good name).

Names ending with *-ing* originally referred only to people but soon came to signify the place where they lived. When we say we are going "to the Joneses", we really mean we are going to their house and garden, and so it was with the *-ing* names. They are found chiefly in the east and south of England where the invading tribes came first. Later on when the invaders were more widely spread they were inclined to add another word to indicate the exact place they were speaking of. So Woking was probably the first encampment of Woca's people, and Wokingham near by a homestead they built a little later.

Here are some typical names with *ing* in the middle; there are hundreds to choose from. Birmingham was the homestead of Beorma's people; Nottingham, the home of Snot and his party. Why Snot? you may ask. We know he was called Snot because the *S* can be seen in the early records. It was only dropped in the Norman period (*snot* in Old English meant wise). Buckingham meant the meadow of Bucca's people—and here it must be explained that the ending *-ham* has another possible origin besides "home", for another word with a different vowel sound, meaning a meadow by a stream, has become confused with it. Only the oldest records can show which is which.

Rottingdean was the valley of Rota's people; Basingstoke the meeting-place of Basa's tribe, who had settled first at Old Basing a few miles away. Paddington and Kensington were the farms of Padda and Kensig and their families; Waddington in the north was the farm of Wada's group—and it must have been a different Wada who had a wooded hill at Wadhurst in Sussex. Many of these names crop up in several places far apart. Gylla, for instance, seems to have been popular; there are three Gillinghams—in Dorset, Kent and Norfolk— all homesteads of men of this name.

There are exceptions to everything, and *-ing* does

not always follow a man's name. Occasionally a group name was formed from the place where the group belonged. The Uppings were "the people of the upland", and their home was Uppingham. (Dartington has already been mentioned on page 37.) Accrington is not really an -*ing* name at all. It was "the acorn farm". Pigs ate acorns and this must have been ideal for them.

In the later Anglo-Saxon period the use of group names faded out and places were spoken of just by their owner's name with a word added to tell what sort of place it was: Edgbaston, Egbert's farm; Alfriston, Aelfric's farm; Ilfracombe, Alfred's valley (it may not sound like it now, but we can see it written as *Alfredes cumbe* in records of 1249).

One thing that is interesting to note is the importance of women among the Anglo-Saxons. On page 32 we mentioned Bebbe, the queen from whom Bamburgh took its name at the end of the sixth century. Not long afterwards Bognor on the south coast is recorded as *Bugganora*; that is, Bugge's shore. You may not care much for Bugge (pronounced as two syllables, like Beb-be) as a girl's name but the king of Wessex of that time had a daughter called Bugge, and it was probably she who owned this bit of coast.

These were royal ladies, but dozens of ordinary women appear also as land-owners all over the country. Kimberley, for instance, was "Cyneburg's lea", and that is a feminine name. Wolverhampton belonged in the tenth century to a lady called

Wulfrun. Before that it had been called just *Heantune*, meaning "high village", but after she had given money to build a church there it became *Wulfrune hanton*. Later still the last part of the name was confused with the more common *hampton*, and finally it all ran together in its present form.

Among the many changes brought by the Norman Conquest was a new style of name-giving. A whole new set of Christian names became popular and have remained so ever since—William, Robert, Richard, John and so on—and because people were beginning to have surnames they could use these fashionable Christian names over and over instead of always searching for something different. This meant that the old Saxon names dropped out of use, except for a very few famous ones, and most of them were quickly forgotten. That is why they have been so much mispronounced, compressed and knocked about in the many place names where they still exist.

Brighton was Beorhthelm's *tun*. This was spelt Brighthelmstone until the early nineteenth century, but the pronunciation had taken a short cut long before. Bakewell was the well or spring of Badeca, whose name was gradually reduced to Bake. Darlington was the farm of Dearnoth's people. You might wonder how that came about; by the time of the Conquest it had come down to Dearningtun, and then perhaps the familiarity of the word "darling" and a bit of joking made the next change easy. Darling is a very old term of affection.

53

Another place name whose origin could not possibly be guessed from the modern form is Elstree. In a charter of A.D. 785 it is mentioned as "Tidwulf's tree", Tidwulf being a man's name. Then when people spoke later on of meeting "at Tidwulf's tree" they began to think that the T sound belonged to "at" (remember that hardly anyone could read or write) and so it became Idulf's tree. It might easily have stuck firm at Iddlestree, but it was squeezed up even further.

It is the presence of these forgotten personal names in our place names that makes so many of them difficult to explain. Yet these curious old names, battered and squashed as they often are, are helpful in giving a great variety. If all our names were like Ashford or Heathfield, we should have no trouble in understanding them, but they would be less fascinating, and far too many of them would be the same.

Then again it is only right that the early makers of the land should have their permanent place in it. Few of them have any other claim to fame. It is not true to say they are remembered in the places that bear their names, for very few people ever think of them, but their names are there if we trouble to look for them.

Beliefs and Customs

THE CHRISTIAN faith first came into Britain in the
time of Roman rule, but it was swept out again by
the Angles and Saxons. However, they did not
conquer the whole island and in the west the Britons
clung to their faith through all their troubles. From
there it spread into Ireland and from there into
Scotland, so that just as it was being extinguished
in the east it was burning more brightly in the west.

In Cornwall the Britons remained a long time in
possession, and although it was included in the
English kingdom by the tenth century it has always
kept its own character. Until two hundred years ago
it had its own language which was very like Welsh,
and most of its place names belong to this Cornish
tongue. Many of them are the names of Cornwall's
own saints, both men and women, who kept the

faith alive in a time of disaster, and were loved in the places where their names live on: St Austell, St Keverne, St Just, St Mawes, and many more.

We know very little of most of these Cornish saints. The local people passed on stories of them but it is hard to pick out the facts from the fancy. St Peran, whose name survives at Perranporth (Peran's port) and Perranzabuloe (Peran-on-the-sands), was supposed to have floated from Ireland on a millstone; while Ia, a Welsh princess who built the church in the harbour we call St Ives (St Ia's), is said to have sailed there on a leaf. We can't believe such tales, but Peran and Ia were probably real people who did found churches in these places and had adventures on the sea.

In most of the rest of England Christianity was for a time blotted out, but names can survive when all else is lost and even in districts entirely settled by the heathen English a few echoes of that first Christianity remain. One such is the name Eccles. It comes from the Latin word *ecclesia* which means a church, and is found in several places where there must have been churches before the coming of the English. They must have heard the word spoken by Britons and treated it as the name of the place.

The English invaders believed in many strange gods and goddesses such as Tiw, Woden, Thor and Frig whose names live on in the days of the week. The one they seem to have thought most of was Woden, the cunning, all-powerful, one-eyed magic-maker. They made temples to him on hills and in woods and, though we know very little of what went on there, we do know the words they used for these temples, words that were never used for any Christian place. One was *hearg* (with the "g" pronounced as a final grunt as in *burg*). This became Harrow. It exists in several places, the best known being Harrow-on-the-Hill. The other word was *weoh* and this makes the beginning of the place names Weedon (temple on a hill), and Weeley (temple in a clearing). There are three places in England called Wellington, and their names probably come from the same word. First there was the *weoh leah* or sacred woodland glade. Then the people who lived near it were called the Weolings; finally *Weolingtun* (as it was spelt in Somerset in 903) was their village. It is a long step from these strange folk to the great Duke who took his title from their place, and from whom many other far-off places have been named.

The worship of Woden and Thor was a fairly brief interlude in our long history, for only about a hundred and fifty years after the first English settlements were made the Christian faith made its second entry into the land—in fact two entries for it came from two directions. In the south St Augustine, sent from Rome, landed in Kent in 597 and began at once to make converts. In the north only a few years later Oswald, king of Northumbria, invited a missionary monk from the island of Iona to come and teach his people. From these two centres the faith spread with amazing speed.

The last part of England to remain heathen was

57

the Midlands, and here there are names that still proclaim the old religion. Wednesfield means Woden's open space, evidently a meeting-place for ceremonies; Wednesbury, not far off, is Woden's stronghold. Further south an ancient earthwork that stretches for miles across country was called Woden's dyke, now Wansdyke. It had been made long before the coming of the English and seemed so strange and wonderful to them that they thought only Woden could have made it. They had a sort of nickname for him too, Grim, and even after they became Christian they still told tales of his mysterious doings under this name. That is why many prehistoric remains have this name attached to them: Grimes Grave, a hollowed-out cave; Grimsdyke, another earthwork like the Wansdyke; and others.

The early English were an outdoor people and their gatherings, whether tribal or religious, were in the open air. The word *stow* which makes part of many place names, meant a meeting-place, both in heathen times and later, and *stoke* was much the same. Plaistow meant "play place", using play in the sense of athletic sports. It sounds like a sort of early stadium. Several places are simply called Stow or Stoke and nothing more, but most of them, like Stowmarket and Stoke-on-Trent, have some later addition.

Although *stow* could be a meeting-place of any kind it was very often a religious one. Godstow was "God's place", Halstow, "holy place"; and once

58

the English were Christian they often combined it with a saint's name. Felixstowe was the place of St Felix, a missionary sent from Kent in the early seventh century to convert the East Anglians. In the west, Bridestowe was St Bride's place, and Padstow the place of Petroc, one of the best known of the Cornish saints. Petroc founded a monastery at Padstow in the sixth century and is said to have died as a hermit on Bodmin Moor. Here another monastery cherished his relics and his memory. Bodmin comes from the Cornish *bod myneich* (house of monks).

The earliest known saint in all Britain is Alban whose name remains unmistakably in the place where he died. He was a Roman soldier stationed in Britain at the time when Christians were being persecuted. He sheltered a Christian priest in the town of Verulamium and for this was executed on a nearby hill. When the Roman rulers themselves became Christian a little later the place of his death was remembered with honour, and even during the dark interlude when the heathen English were in possession it was not forgotten. When the English accepted the same faith they built a church on the hill-top and called the place Albanstow. Many pilgrims came there and it grew into a busy town, while the ruins of the Roman city below the hill disappeared under earth and grass. Later came the Normans who replaced the Saxon church with a great cathedral. They spoke of it as St Alban's and the Old English *-stow* was dropped.

On the whole the English had much less tendency than the Britons to call their villages after saints, and only did so when the saintly person was very important in that region. A saintly king whose name lives in his own kingdom is Oswald of Northumbria, though some of the places in the north that contain this name may refer to other Oswalds. We have no proof, for instance, to connect him personally with Oswaldtwistle (Oswald's point of land between two streams), but Oswestry (Oswald's tree) does seem to be the spot on which he was killed in battle in 641. In Old English the word "tree" was often used for a tall wooden cross set up in the ground. We know it had this meaning here because the Welsh name for this place is *Croesoswald* (Oswald's cross). We are told that many pilgrims visited the place where the king fell, and so it is likely it was marked with some memorial.

This brings to mind some other town names that end in *-tree*. Nearly all begin with the name of a man. Coventry was Cofa's tree; Daventry, Dafa's tree; Braintree, Elstree and Manningtree are the same type of name again. One wonders whether some of these were crosses as at Oswestry, memorials perhaps to honoured men, or were they meeting-places for tribal groups of which Cofa and the rest were the leaders? Unfortunately there are no answers to these questions. But we do know that special trees often marked the spots for important gatherings. Matlock, for instance, means "meeting oak".

As soon as the English became Christian they began building churches and monasteries all over the land, and although nearly all were rebuilt in later times the places where they stood were sacred and almost never changed. "Church" is an easy word to recognize in place names, but the priest, who was just as important, may go unnoticed. Preston means the priest's farm. Prestcot is the priest's cottage.

Minster means a monastic church, generally of Saxon origin. There were many small monasteries in Saxon England, generally beside rivers so that the monks could catch plenty of fish. Sturminster was on the Stour, Exminster on the Exe and so on; but Kidderminster, on the other hand, begins with a man's name—it was the minster of Cydela, perhaps the first abbot.

Many minsters, however, took over names that were there long before they were built. Jarrow, for instance, was the name of a tribe who had settled there in heathen times. It was here that the monk Bede (A.D. 673–735) wrote his history of the English Church, which is the earliest account that we have of Anglo-Saxon England. This is one of our chief sources for early place names.

In the centuries after the Norman Conquest the church grew rich. Wealth in those days meant the possession of much land; whole villages, and many of them, belonged to abbots and bishops. So when old village names needed more description, as they often did, and owners' titles were added to them, this often resulted in names like Abbots Langley and Bishops Waltham.

Another way to differentiate villages of the same name was to add the names of the saints to whom their churches were dedicated as at Gussage All Saints and Gussage St Michael (Gussage means "gushing stream"). But late additions of this sort are very different from the names of places like Felixstowe or St Ives where the root and origin of the place name is the memory of a saintly man or woman who had actually lived or died in that spot.

The Vikings

THE ENGLISH people had been Christian for about two centuries and were progressing in the arts of peace when a new invasion from the sea fell on them. The heathen Danes, coming in their long boats, terrible with their horned helmets and battle axes, were very like what the English themselves had been four centuries earlier. But that was no comfort to them now.

However this time events turned out differently. The English in their invasion had swept on in a conquering wave as far as the western coasts of the island, stopped only by the Welsh in their mountains and the more northern Britons allied with the Scots. The Danes came close to conquering much of England, but then King Alfred of Wessex beat them in battle, drove them back and wisely made peace with them, agreeing that they might settle in the north-east if they would become Christian. This was not really the end of the matter for later on more Danes made more attacks, but Alfred had saved England from complete disaster.

All this had a great effect on our place names, for in the Danelaw, as the north-eastern part of the country was called for a time, thousands of Danes made their permanent homes and named their settlements in their own words.

The regular Danish word for a farm or village was *by*. This corresponds to the English *tun*, and ends hundreds of village names in the north-east counties. You have only to look for the places ending in *-by* on the map to tell how thickly a district was settled by Danes. (This word has passed into Modern English in just one expression—bye-laws, the laws of the town.)

Another Danish word for a farm, generally a small offshoot from the main one, was *thorp*, a common ending in the north and one that often stands alone as Thorpe. Other typical Danish words in our place names are: *thwaite* (a clearing or meadow), *garth* (an enclosed place), *fell* (a steep hill) and *gill* (a deep valley).

But although the Danes brought some new words into England their language on the whole was very close to English. Many words were just the same, or as near as made no difference. For instance, both had the word "ness" for a cape (it really meant a nose), but the English did not use it very often, being more inclined to call a jutting-out piece of land a "head". Foulness, "birds' headland", was so called by the English, but the Danes used the word very freely on all the coasts they raided. Thorpeness is a Danish "headland with a farm".

Again the English knew the word "dale" for a valley but far more often called it a "dene". It was the Danes who called all the great valleys of the north dales, generally combining the word with the name of the river that ran down the dale. So we have Dovedale, Allendale, Airedale and so on. The river names are far older than the Danish settlement; some of them are prehistoric.

The Danish word for an island was almost the same as the English. They make the common place name endings -ey and -y; and so does the English word for a river; so that all one can say about these endings is that they are watery. But the Danes had a distinctive word of their own, *holm*, for a flat-topped island.

In time the two languages merged together into one northern speech, and many names are a mixture of the two. Appleby, Selby and Willoughby, all farms named from trees—apple, sallow and willow —have the typical Danish ending but English tree-names. Ashby, very common in the north, is the Danish form of Ashton.

There had always been differences of pronunciation between the different regions of England and the Danish settlers made them stronger. Some can be clearly seen in place names. For instance, the

E

sounds of "sh" and "ch" (as we write them now) became hard "sk" and "k" sounds in the north. Thus Skipton in Yorkshire has the same meaning (sheep farm) as Shipton further south. Skelton is the northern form of Shelton (farm on a shelf— that is, a flat ledge on a hillside). And Carlton is the twin of Charlton (the churls' farm—a churl or a carl was a free man but not of noble birth).

One more pair of words of this sort is "church" and "kirk". The Danish invaders began by burning down the "kirks", as they called them, but learned to value them later when they had become Christian. How much is shown by the number of villages called Kirkby, often shortened to Kirby. There were so many that most of these names had to have a later addition to distinguish them, such as Kirby-moorside or Kirby Lonsdale (Lonsdale is the valley of the Lune).

The Danish pirates were a rough, tough crowd who often called each other by rude nicknames. Just as the English did, they named many places from the men who lived there, and so these nick-names remain on the land. Skegness was the cape of Skeggi, the "bearded"; they probably all had beards and so his must have been remarkable. Scunthorpe was the farm of Skuma, the "squinter"; Londesborough was the fort of Lothinn, the "hairy"; Slingsby, the village of Slenger, the "idler"; Scarborough, the fort of Skarthi, the "hare-lipped"; and Broclesby, the village of Broclos, who had lost his breeches. They made nicknames from animals too

66

as the English did. Ormskirk, for example, belonged to Orm, and that means "snake" or "dragon".

It must not be thought that the Danes renamed all the places where they settled. On the whole they kept old names, making new ones chiefly for their own settlements. An exception is Derby which had formerly been Northworthy (north farm). The Danes called it Derby (deer farm) from the herds of deer that they found there.

But old names that survived might be greatly changed by Danish speech. A famous name that was much altered in this way is York. It was a Brittonic name, old before the Romans came there: they wrote it *Eboracum* (which is why the Archbishop of York still signs himself *Ebor*). Its root is a Celtic word meaning a yew tree, though the exact form here seems to have meant "place of Eburos"— the name perhaps of a man or of a spirit of the trees. We know that the Celtic people worshipped many gods, some connected with rivers, some with ancient trees. Their priests, the Druids, performed strange ceremonies in groves of yews or oaks, and Eboracum was probable one of those.

But that is only the beginning. The Romans did not have the "v" sound in their language. They used this letter to represent the sound of "w" or "u", and when they heard a "v" sound in Celtic names they wrote it as "b" (this may seem very odd to us, but try saying "b" with your lips not quite closed and you will find how very near it can be to "v"). So *Eboracum* was really *Evoracum*, and

67

the -*um* was a Latin ending which did not last after the Romans had gone.

Next came the Angles who, hearing something like *Evorac*, confused it with their own word *eofor* and made the name into *Eoforwic* which would mean "wild-boar village". Then much later again, the Danes captured the town and made it their headquarters. In their speech its name was shortened first to *Iorvik*, and finally to a single short, sharp sound, more like the bark of a dog than a gracious name—York. And that does not end its story. Just think of its namesakes all over the world, beginning with New York.

The Danish invasion of England was only one part of a greater movement. It was as if Scandinavia exploded in the ninth century. While Danes were pouring into England, daring men of the same sort were setting out also from the fiords of Norway in their open boats to harry the coasts of Scotland, Ireland and France. They colonized the Shetlands, the Orkneys, and the Isle of Man; they reached Iceland and Greenland (which are named in their tongue) and even North America which they called Vinland. Their exploits were incredible.

Those who came from Norway were called Northmen, and some of the places where they settled in England became Normanton and Normanby, as compared with Danby (Danes' village). But they were also called Vikings, because they came from the sheltered inlets where their ships could lie at anchor, and their word for such an inlet

68

was *vik*. We will meet them again in later chapters when we come to the place names of Scotland, Ireland and Wales, but we must think of them now not only invading England from the east but sweeping right round and raiding in the west too. All the islands whose names end in -*holm*, Flatholm, Grassholm, and the rest, were once theirs; all the Skerries, here and there, are simply "rocks" in their language, and Lundy Island preserves their word *lundi* for a puffin.

Even on the south coast of England where the Vikings have left few traces, they had at least one regular anchorage. The little Cornish port of Helford is not really by an English "ford" but on a "fiord", the Northman's word for a narrow inlet. The first syllable is the Cornish *hayle*, meaning salt water, and the so-called Helford River is not a true river but, as its name implies, a briny inlet.

The Northmen made use of the Channel Islands too. The names Jersey, Guernsey and Alderney all end with one of their regular words for an island. But the first parts of these names, together with Sark, Herm and Jethou, are of unknown origin—possibly Celtic. Though the islands were inhabited from prehistoric times there are few clear records of them before the Norman period.

Although the Northmen used all the islands round Britain as bases they were more attracted to the richer plunder to be found on mainlands, and France suffered as much as England from their raids. Soon after the year 900 they established a territory of their own on the coast of France which became known as the "Northmen's land" or, in French, *Normandie*. The Vikings who settled there intermarried with the French and learned French skills and arts and the French language, so that when they invaded England more than a century later, led by their powerful ruler William the Conqueror, they were more like Frenchmen than Northmen, though that is the meaning of "Normans". Meanwhile they had kept a grip on the Channel Islands—which are still called *Les Iles Normandes* in French—and that is why most of the names there belong to the French language.

The Normans

THE VIKING raids that had lasted, off and on, for two hundred years were brought to an end when the Normans conquered England. They too were of Viking origin but they had been so long settled in France that they had forgotten their northern language and spoke nothing but French when they invaded England.

When William of Normandy had staked all his chances on the battle near Hastings and by it won himself a kingdom, his chief act of gratitude for his victory was the building of an abbey on the site of the battle; but he invented no high-sounding name for it; it was simply Battle Abbey, and the little town that grew up around it became Battle, a plain, stark fact with no frills.

"Battle" and "abbey" are two of the many words

of French origin that came into England by force of arms at that time. Castle, tower, forest, lake, river, mountain, even village and farm—all these were new words to the English, thrust into their speech by the Normans. They came too late to make a basic part in many place names, for the land was fully named already, but often they have been added to the old names as separate words, repeating the meaning that was already there. When we say *River Avon*, *Lake* Winder*mere*, West*minster Abbey*, Sher*wood Forest* and so forth, the meaning of the extra word was already there in the old name.

The Normans did not come as a great wave of new settlers as the Danes had done, but they seized the reins of power and ruled an unwilling people. They took over the country as they found it and this included its names. They might mispronounce them, and add extra words to them, but few old names disappeared at this time except where whole villages were deliberately wiped out, as in the wide tract that they called the New Forest.

And on the whole the Normans did not make many completely new names. But they were great builders of abbeys and castles, and when they built one in a place where nothing in particular had been before—as at Battle—they did name it in their own language. Some of these names still have a foreign look though we have generally given them a thoroughly English sound. The Normans may have distorted some of our names, but we have done the same to theirs.

Here are a few French names given soon after the Conquest. Beaulieu means "beautiful place"; the French spelling has been preserved in Hampshire, but it is pronounced "Bewley", and that is the way it is spelt in Kent. The same name has gone one step further in Worcestershire as Bewdley. Belper was *beau repaire*, "fair retreat", and Beachey Head, which sounds so English, was *beau chef*, "fair headland". The French used *chef*, meaning "head", exactly as the English did for a cape, but the local people, not understanding that, reduced *Beau chef* to Beachey and added their own "Head" to make things clear.

A few more French names. Grampound in Cornwall was *grand pont*, "big bridge"; Mold, just over the Welsh border, was *mont haut*, "high hill"; Freemantle in Hampshire was *froid mantel*, "cold cloak", a fanciful name for a wood; and Haltemprice, "high endeavour", a moral name for a new abbey. Another name that includes the Old French word for "high" is Haltwhistle. The second part of this place name is the Old English *twisla* used for land in the fork of a river. A Norman landowner must have called this place "the high fork", but now after long use it sounds more like a direction to passing trains.

The tendency of the Normans to make up new names praising the beauty of the landscape or expressing high ideals was a new thing in England. Old English place names and Danish ones too consist of plain facts telling just what a place was or who lived there with no comments on prettiness or moral aims.

Another habit of the Normans when building castles in England was to call them after their homes in Normandy. It was not done very often because castles were generally built in places which already had old names which they simply carried on. William the Conqueror, for instance, building his fine new castle at Windsor was content with the name he found there, humble though it was (page 39), and probably never gave it a thought. But a few barons did transplant names from across the channel; one of these is Richmond.

The story of Richmond begins in Normandy with the village of *Richemont* ("rich" or "royal" hill). When William I's cousin, Count Alan of Brittany, built himself a new castle high on a cliff in Yorkshire he chose to give it this fine French name. William made him Earl of Richmond; and four hundred years later another Earl of Richmond came to the throne as Henry VII. He built himself a palace near London which took its name from his title. So Richmond-on-Thames is a rather late name with a roundabout history.

A name brought from much farther off and unique in England is Baldock. Although it sounds so English it is actually the Norman version of Baghdad. During the reign of William I many Norman knights joined in the First Crusade, to try and free the Holy Land from the Turks. Among them were a group called the Knights Templar, who owned land in many parts of England. Those who returned from the Crusade brought back memories of the strange cities they had seen, though they did not always speak or spell their names correctly. They wrote Baghdad as *Baldac*, but why one of them gave this exotic name to his manor in Hertfordshire we can only guess. Perhaps as a joke because it was so different.

Occasionally a new castle was called by the name of the man who built it. Barnard Castle and Richards Castle, both built by Normans, sound very modern compared with the ancient castle names like Cadbury and Badbury, and so they are. Another name that tells of a castle or fortified house with its Norman owner is Bloomsbury. We hear of it in 1280 as *Blemondes beri* when it belonged to a family called de Blemond. Although their surname was French they had evidently learned English as they called their home a "bury".

That is what happened to the proud Normans in the course of time. They married English girls and after a few generations they were speaking English. For two hundred years the official language of the court was French but the great mass of the people never learned to speak it, and it was English that triumphed in the end.

William the Conqueror was a great organizer and extremely efficient. He gave out the land among his barons (keeping plenty for himself) but he was determined to tax them for what they had and therefore he ordered the great survey that is known as Domesday Book. This was made in 1086. It still exists and is one of the most valuable sources we have for the origins of our names, for it lists almost all the towns, villages and even farms of England as they were at that time. Many of our names are on record much earlier than that, but this fills the gaps.

It was the businesslike habits of the Norman kings that caused so many of our village names to have second names added to them. In the Anglo-Saxon period the people had been much freer to manage their own affairs, and a simple name like Stoke was quite sufficient in its own district. But now the king's clerks made lists of taxes due from all parts of the land, and when the same names appeared in different places something more had to be added to distinguish them. Very often that something was the name of the new owner, and the chances were that he was a Norman.

It was just at this time that the leading Norman families were beginning to use surnames. Some of these came from their nicknames. We can see examples in Shepton Mallet, Wootton Bassett, and Leighton Buzzard: William Malet, who fought at Hastings, received his from the hammerlike club that he swung in battle; bassett means "short"; a buzzard is a kind of hawk, and the man who earned this nickname was fierce and strong.

Many barons had surnames derived from the villages in Normandy that they came from. These make the second parts of various place names: Melton Mowbray, Milton Keynes, Stoke Mandeville, Stoke Poges and many more. Most of them have suffered some change by use in England. The Mowbrays originally came from *Montbrai*, the Keynes from a place called *Cahagnes*, and the owners of Stoke Poges from *le Pugeis*. Ashby de la Zouche was held in 1200 by Roger de la Zuche. His surname came from a French word meaning a tree stump which must have named the farm or village where his family had lived. It would be wrong to explain Ashby de la Zouche as meaning "ash farm of the stump", for the ash grew in England and the stump was in Normandy and both may have been dead and gone before the two names were brought together.

In all these examples the first name is plain English and found in many places. Melton is generally the middle farm, Milton one that had a mill (but there has been some confusion between these two), and Stoke was explained on page 58. If they had not been common they would not have needed extra tags. But the tags add charm and variety. They are echoes from the conquering army of Hastings, the barons who built their castles to dominate the land, but later lost their links with France and became English.

10

The Last Seven Centuries

FROM 1200 to 1300 was an important century for
England. It began with King John losing all his
French possessions so that from then on her kings
were kings of England only. And it was in that
century that the English language, which ever since
the Conquest had been spoken by the people but
not by their rulers, and hardly ever written down,
emerged again as the official language. It had
changed greatly during its time of obscurity; it had
been enriched by many French words; its grammar
was simplified, and its spelling more modern. In
fact it was much nearer to the language we speak
today. Place names coined after about 1300 are
generally easy for us to understand.

But actually the making of new names had
slackened off, for every bit of England had its name.

Villages were growing into towns, and new farms starting where there had been only woods or pools before, but the names were there ready for them. Liverpool, for instance, is not in Domesday Book, presumably because it was not worth mentioning in 1086. The name means "muddy pool" and perhaps it was nothing more than that, but when a settlement grew around it the name was there. That is the way of English place names. They are often older than the towns they name.

The chief changes in place names since about 1300 have been made by adding still more to the old ones. At the same time the process of wearing them down by continual use has gone on too; but there has been more lengthening than shortening.

Double names have been mentioned many times already; indeed one cannot write about English names without them; they are so plentiful and picturesque. In the last chapter we collected some in which the extra words were the names of Norman owners. But it was not only Normans who were making these additions. The English were doing it too; in fact they had always done it, building up names from the simplest beginnings. But in early times the new word had always joined on to what was there before, still keeping a single-word name. The *tun* became *hamtun*, and then much later one of the Hamptons became Northampton and another Southampton. When a village called Eaton came into the possession of a nunnery soon after the Conquest, it became Nuneaton. But after about

1300 when extra words were added to a place's name they remained separate.

Often these extra words were just descriptive. Stony Stratford and Fenny Stratford, two river-crossings on the same Roman road, had different troubles. Over Wallop was higher up the hill than Nether Wallop. A great many describe the situations: Stow-on-the-Wold, Wotton-under-Edge, Barton-in-the-Beans, and other pleasant names explain themselves.

A curious hangover from the Norman period is the little French word *le* which comes in the middle of some of these phrase-names, sandwiched absurdly between two English words: Newton-le-Willows, Bolton-le-Sands, Hutton-le-Hole, and so on. These all began like the other place names, simply stating in English where the places were, but French-speaking clerks tended to translate the little connecting words into French, writing *en le* for "in the". Then to save time they reduced it to *le* only. So that was how the names appeared in writing and after a time the local people began to say them like that.

Here are a few double names that might be puzzling. In Saffron Walden the older part is Walden, the "Welsh dene" or valley of the Britons; later on it was known for the saffron that grew wild there, a plant much valued in cookery for its flavour and colour. Chipping Norton was noted for its market: Chipping comes from an Old English word for buying and selling, and makes part of many place names, such as Cheapside and Chepstow, but has dropped out of the living language, ousted by "market" which began as a French word.

Queen Camel, which sounds so comic, began as a Celtic name. *Cam* in the British language meant "curved" or "winding" and several river names begin with it, including the Camel in Cornwall. The village probably took its name from a stream; then long afterwards Edward I gave it to his wife, Queen Eleanor. Some other village names that refer to owners are Earls Barton (this belonged to the Earl of Huntingdon), Child Okeford (*"child"* was often used for a noble youth), and Maids Moreton, which must have been the inheritance of a young girl.

When "king" is part of a one-word name such as Kingston or Kingsley it is fairly sure that the place belonged to one of the Anglo-Saxon kings, but when it is added as a separate word it is of a later date. Kings Lynn refers to Henry VIII who dissolved the monastery there and kept all its property for himself. Lynn is a Brittonic word, the same as the Welsh *llyn*, meaning a lake or pool. As this town is on the east coast where the Angles landed in the fifth century, it must have been then that they heard the name *Lynn* and adopted it. That means that more than a thousand years separate the two parts of this name.

After the king the greatest landowners in the Middle Ages were the church authorities, and many village names (as we noted on page 61) tell of priors, canons, bishops and abbots to whom the villagers had to pay their rents. But the most curious result of so much church ownership is the scattering of Latin words around the countryside. The monks kept their accounts in Latin, and in listing the manors on an abbey estate would translate as much as possible into that language. The old village names were generally left as they were, but the supporting words were translated. So we have odd mixtures like Sheepy Magna and Sheepy Parva. *Magna* and *parva* are Latin for "great" and "little". They seem very out of place beside the simple old English Sheepy, which means "sheep island".

It was among small villages where the influence of local monasteries loomed large that the longest Latin tags stuck fast. Here are a few with their tags translated: Kingsbury *Episcopi*, "of the bishop" (it had been a king's fort long before); Whitchurch *Canonicorum*, "of the canons"; Ashby *Puerorum*, "of the boys" (the rents from this village paid for the upkeep of the Lincoln choir-boys); Zeal *Monachorum*, "of the monks" (Zeal is the Wessex pronunciation of sallow, a kind of willow); Toller *Porcorum*, "of the pigs" (Toller is a Celtic river-name, and this village was called Swine Toller before the monks got to work).

We must not for a moment confuse this late monkish Latin of the Middle Ages with the living Latin spoken by the Romans when they were in Britain. From that live language many words such as "street" and "port" came indirectly into English, by way of the Britons, to become basic parts of our modern speech. The odd bits stuck on by monastic landowners hundreds of years later are a very different matter. They are not really numerous, but very noticeable because they are so out of place and comical.

We have gone on adding bits to our place names ever since, even up to the present day, to make them fit changing conditions. We have even sometimes added a Latin word because it seemed in the right tradition. When George V stayed at Bognor after an illness in 1929 its people proudly added *Regis* to their town's name. Regis means "of the king" and was often used in earlier times to indicate royal property.

But more usually we add plain English words—East and West, Upper and Lower, and so on—to indicate new suburbs of growing towns or new subdivisions. They are not so picturesque as some of the old additions, but who knows what will seem quaint in a few more centuries? When the people living near two villages called Hadham (farm in the heath) began to call the larger one Much Hadham they were only using their normal word for "big", but now we think it amusing.

One word that has been used to very good effect in modern times to cope with the huge growth of built-up areas is "side". Almost every city is on a river and when it has spread along the banks engulfing other towns and villages we use the river name with this useful word for the whole district. So such names as Merseyside, Tyneside, Teesside and Humberside have grown as naturally as any of the old ones and are there ready and waiting for the new counties and county boroughs that have been made. Far from being new names, they have grown out of some of the oldest ones we have.

In this century many new towns have been deliberately planned and quickly built, a thing that has never happened on this scale before. But nearly all of them have carried on the names that were there before. For there always is a name. You couldn't find a site in England big enough even for a village with no name on it. One of the first new towns was Welwyn Garden City, and in this case the planners simply used the name of the old village close to their site (Welwyn means "the willows") with two new words added. "City" was not a good choice, for the place is not a city in the proper meaning of the word, and already the local people are inclined to call it simply Welwyn and the original village Old Welwyn, which seems the more natural way to distinguish them.

Since then over twenty more new towns have been built and almost all have carried on old names that were there before. Only for two of them have new ones been devised and this was not for lack of names but because two or more villages were being swallowed up in one town and it was hard to choose between them. Peterlee was named from a man, Peter Lee, who had been a leader of the miners in that district in hard times. Telford in Shropshire

84

was named in honour of Thomas Telford, the famous engineer, who was at one time surveyor of that county. These two names are completely outside the English tradition of naming. Different lands have different styles and in the younger countries overseas towns are often named as tributes to men, but the English habit has always been otherwise.

It is true that many of our old town names contain the names of men, but only because it was natural to speak of the place in that way. Biggleswade was a place where you could wade across a stream and it belonged to Bigel, as stated. It was not a tribute to him but a fact. Most English people prefer the old names that have this sort of historic truth to anything newly made-up, and fortunately there is seldom need for new ones.

I am thinking of course of the more important names: those of cities, towns, villages, rivers, hills and districts. If there were room to write also of the minor names of fields, roads, private houses, schools and so on it would be a different story for when it comes to such matters there is plenty of modern invention—there has to be with so much new building; but there are old names in this class too, and they are always worth preserving.

11

Wales

WELSH IS, by a long way, the senior living language of Britain. In an earlier form it was spoken right across the island for nearly a thousand years before the coming of the English. Its words, as we have frequently noticed, remain embedded like fossils in English place names. In Wales they are part of a living language.

To the Romans Britain was all one land and in the part that later became Wales they built forts as they did elsewhere, using for them the native names that they found on the spot. As their forts were mostly on rivers they were called by river names. Conway, for instance, is the Welsh *Conwy*, "glorious river". The Romans wrote it *Conovium*, but when you remember that they used the letter "v" for the sound of "w", and that *-um* was a regular Latin ending that would drop off later, you can see it is the same.

Another of their forts was on the Neath river which in Welsh means "shining". The Romans, having no letter for the "th" sound, wrote it *Nidum*. They also knew the island of Mon (Anglesey in English) and fought a great battle with the Druids there. They called it *Mona*. Mon is a mysterious name closely connected with Man. Some scholars think that both these island names come in some way from Manannan, the ancient Celtic god of the sea.

The Romans knew Carmarthen as *Moridun(um)*, "fort by the sea". *Mor* is still "sea" in Welsh, and *dun* was the earlier Brittonic word for a fort. In time Moridun became Marddin and then the local people, forgetting its meaning, added another word for a fortress, *caer*; so it became Carmarthen, literally "fort sea-fort".

Most of the Welsh names beginning with *Caer-* (or *Car-* which is how the English often spell it) have famous castles, as the word tells us. Caerleon means "fortress of the legions": the Romans had a great military centre there, but left it fifteen hundred years ago. Cardiff is "the castle on the Taff" (the "dark river").

Because the Welsh are descended from the Britons who lived under Roman rule they have many Latin words in their language. One is *pont*, a bridge. Pontypool means the bridge by the pool. The "y" in the middle is Welsh for "the", but in place names it can mean "of the" or "by the" or whatever is appropriate. Pontypridd is the bridge by the house-made-of-earth. Pont-y-pant is the bridge in the valley.

Another Welsh word of Latin origin is *eglwys*, a church, from *ecclesia*. Eglwysbach is "little church". But the Welsh had a word of their own that they used much more. *Eglwys* means only the church, but *llan* was originally church and churchyard, the whole sacred enclosure. The beginning *Llan-* is as common in Wales as the ending *-ton* in England and this tells us something about the two races; for the English thought most of their farms, but to the Welsh the heart of each village was its holy place.

When Roman rule had ended and the surviving Britons were driven into the west they were for a time divided into several kingdoms and some of the names of the princes who ruled in that obscure period still remain in the places where they once held power. Merioneth was the land of Meirion, and Cardigan of Ceredig, royal brothers of the house of Gwynneth, the northern kingdom. Brecon takes its name from Brychan, a sixth-century ruler famous for his large family, many of whom were remembered as saints. (The maiden Ia who founded St Ives in Cornwall is said to have been one of his many daughters.) Further south reigned several successive princes of the name of Morgan, and Glamorgan means Morgan's shore.

But much as the Welsh honoured their princes,

their strongest love was given to the holy men—
and women too—who seemed blessed with divine
power. These Celtic saints, who belong equally to
Wales, Cornwall, Brittany, Ireland and Scotland,
for they were always sailing in their flimsy little
boats from one to another of these rocky shores, are
mostly very obscure. Many fanciful tales were told
of their adventures but few hard facts have been
preserved. Yet most of them were real people, truly
remembered for a time in the places where their
names remain. And they are found chiefly in the
place names that begin with *Llan-*.

There are hundreds of names that begin in this
way. Some tell where the church was built:
Llandovery is the church on the waters; Llandaff,
by the River Taff; but in the great majority *Llan-*
is followed by the name of a saint. Llangollen,
Llandudno and Llanberis were the churches of
Collen, Tudno and Peris, who were all probably
hermits in those places, but hardly anything is
really known of them. Llanbadarn was founded by
Padarn, a companion and helper of St David, and
Llanelli honours Elli, a holy maiden and yet another
of Brychan's daughters.

St David himself, a very real bishop of the sixth
century, is remembered chiefly in the little city that
in English is called St Davids, where he founded a
monastery. In Welsh it is *Ty Dewi*, Dewi's house.
His proper Welsh name is also to be found in several
villages called Llanddewi.

Llanddeusant means the church of two saints,

Llantrisant of three saints, Llanpumpsant of five saints (these are five of the sons of Brychan who are said to lie sleeping there, and when they wake Wales will return to her former glory).

Welsh is an expressive and poetical language but a difficult one to learn because it is so unlike any other except the only other Celtic survivals, Breton and Gaelic. Few English people ever try to learn it, but with very little effort you can master enough to see the meaning of many of its place names and pronounce them properly. The first hurdle to overcome is the spelling, but this is not nearly as hard as it seems. It looks difficult because a few letters represent different sounds from those they have in English, but these can be soon learnt. Once you have done that you can say any Welsh name with confidence, for the spelling is quite consistent, something we can't claim for English.

The chief differences are these: "dd" is pronounced like "th"; "w" is like "u" (*cwm* is the same as coombe in sound and meaning); "u" is like "i" as in "did"; and "ll" is a special sound something like "thl". "F" is sounded like "v", and "ff" like "f", and if you think this is confusing just consider "of" and "off" in which we do the same thing. This is a helpful point to remember; it makes it clear, for instance, that the English name Avon and the Welsh *afon*, a river, are one and the same.

The second hurdle is called mutation and is much harder to get over. It means that certain words change their first letters according to what has gone before them. Thus *mawr* meaning "big" is sometimes *fawr*; and *bach*, "little", can also be *fach*. This is hard to get used to, but without some glimmering of it you cannot understand Welsh names. When you can recognize that *fynydd* is the same word as *mynydd* (a mountain), you will have gone a long way. ("M" to "F" is one of the regular changes.)

If you look again at the *Llan-* names given on page 89 you will see that the first letters of the saints' names have changed when they follow *Llan*. One of the commonest village names in Wales is Llanfair. This means St Mary's church, for *Mair* has become *fair* (pronounced "vair") in this position.

Now you can understand that Caernarvon is the castle opposite Mon (Anglesey). *Mon* has become *fon*, but is generally spelt with a "v" as a sop to the English.

The names of the best-known Welsh towns nearly all have English forms, some only slightly different from the Welsh, some completely so, and it is reasonable to use these when speaking English. Lampeter is the English version of *Llanbedr* (St Peter's church). Denbigh and Tenby are both *Din bych* (little fort) in Welsh, but Tenby is generally called *Dinbych y Pisgod* (little fort of fishing). Pembroke means land's end. In Welsh it is *Penfro*. The Normans planted a colony here soon after their conquest of England and "Pembroke" was what they made of the Welsh name which then, in its older form, was *Pen brog*.

The Welsh name of Snowdon is *Yr Wyddfa* (pronounced Withva), "the look-out".

The Normans contributed a few French names in places where they built castles, such as Beaumaris (beautiful marshland) and Montgomery which took the name of its builder, Roger of Montgomerie (in Normandy), but more often the castles that they built carried on the names that were there before.

The Vikings too had left some typical names along the coast. The Great Orm's Head means "the dragon's head" in their language. Swansea is "Sweyn's island" and Fishguard "the fishers' garth" or enclosure. Even Milford Haven, which looks so English, is another legacy from the Vikings. The first syllable is not "mill" but *melr*, a "sandbank", the second not a ford but *fiord*, and Haven is the Norse *hafn*, "a harbour". It is a harbour in a fiord with a sandbank.

But in spite of a sprinkling of foreign names along its coasts and near the border the great mass of place names in Wales belong purely to its own language, and except for the saints' names most of them are descriptions of the natural landscape. As in England, rivers play a large part in the naming, and the beginning *Aber-* is very prominent. This means a river-mouth or a place where two streams join. Aberdovey is the mouth of the Dovey (black water) ; Aberdare, of the oak-tree river. Aberystwyth stands at the mouth of the *Ystwyth* (winding river) and Abergavenny at the junction of the Gafenni with the Usk. These last three river names were all known to the Romans. Rhondda is a river name meaning "the loud one", while the Ebbw is thought to mean "wild horses". Cwmbran means valley of the Bran, "the raven river"—and so we might go on.

A list of the Welsh words most frequently found in place names appears on pages 171–172. This should help you to understand many names that you may see in Wales, but remember that in contrast to English the noun generally comes first and descriptive detail after. Here are a few well-known names that are mostly descriptive: Pwllheli, pool of salt water; Harlech, fine slab of stone; Barry, hill brook; Tal y llyn, hillside by a lake; Rhayader, waterfall; Dolgellau, meadow of the cells (probably of monks); Maesteg, fair field; Rhuddlan, red bank; Brynmawr, big hill; Penmaenmawr, head of the big stone; Penrhyndeudraeth, end of the cape with two beaches.

Welsh names are full of rocks, rivers, hills and valleys, and memories of saints.

12

Scotland

THE PLACE names of Scotland are full of mysteries. The early history of the land is so confused and the early records so scanty that it is useless to expect them all to be explained. But the few early accounts that we have of it show many of its names to have been there in ancient times.

The first reports of Scotland come from Greek navigators before the birth of Christ, who sailed all round Albion (as they then called Britain) and threaded their way among cold and misty islands that seemed incredibly far from the civilized world. They must have landed sometimes and spoken with the inhabitants for they heard names that they reported in Greece, and later when the scholar Ptolemy wrote a book about geography, he gave names and positions for *Orcas*, *Hebudes*, *Sketos* and

Mallaos, which must be the islands we know as Orkney, Hebrides, Skye and Mull. *Orcas* may have meant "the island of swine", or possibly "of whales" which were sometimes called sea-pigs in ancient times; its last syllable, the *-ey*, is the Danish word for an island added much later. But the other names are among the mysteries.

There was no separate name for Scotland in those days; it was just part of Albion, and when the Romans began calling the island Britannia the people of the north still used the older name, in the form of Alban or Albany, for their territory. The region called Breadalbane means "uplands of Alban", and in later times the chief title of the eldest son of the king of Scotland was Duke of Albany. This name has been reproduced in England and overseas but few people understand its origin.

The Romans who ruled Britain for four hundred years never conquered the extreme north and in the end they gave up trying and built a wall instead to keep the northern people out. These were the Picts, another mystery. They were fierce fighters as the Romans discovered, but they left no written records that can be understood and it is not even known what language they spoke. Of course they had names for all the places they knew and some of them must have survived. So when a Scottish name can't be explained one always wonders, "Is it Pictish?"

The Britons who occupied the Lowlands at the time of the Roman invasion belonged to the same race as those who survived in Wales, and their place names were made from the same words, such as *Aber-*, a river-mouth, and *Pen-*, a headland or end of a hill. Aberdeen (earlier *Aberdon*) is at the mouth of the Don, a Celtic river name that occurs in several places. Penicuik means "cuckoo hill". *Ros-*, which can mean a headland, like *Pen-*, or simply rough moorland, is common in all the Celtic lands from Cornwall to Scotland, and in Ireland too. It has named a whole Scottish county, Ross, and in the west of England the name of Ross-on-Wye has the same origin.

When the Anglo-Saxons invaded Britain the Angles established the kingdom of Northumbria (land "north of the Humber") and from there spread westwards to Chester and northwards as far as the Firth of Forth. There on a hill near the sea was a British fort called *Eidin*, "steep hill". We know about it because a British bard who was there in about the year 600 wrote a poem describing the young warriors of Eidin feasting and preparing for battle. But they were defeated. The Angles captured Eidin and held it for a time, adding their own word *-burg* to it. So it became Edinburgh, Celtic hill and English fortress.

About the same time as the Angles (or English) were pushing up from the south, another race was invading from the west (Map 1, page 18). These were the Scots from Ireland. It is most confusing for them to have started by being Irish, but that is how it was. For centuries Roman writers called Ireland

Scotia and when large numbers from that country migrated first into the "Scottish" islands and then to the mainland they were generally referred to as the Scots. Actually they were more inclined to speak of themselves as Gaels, and the part of the mainland where they settled first became known as *Airer Gaedel*, the coast of the Gaels. This is now Argyll.

These Scots, or Gaels, were full of energy and creative spirit. It was they who welded together the different races of the north into one kingdom, which took its name from them, and drove the Northumbrians out of Edinburgh. In their own Gaelic language a castle was a *dun*, and they called it *Dun Edin*, but the large numbers of Angles who remained in the Lowlands went on saying Edinburgh.

In the continuous movement of Scots from Ireland to Scotland the person we know most about is St Columba. He was a prince who chose to leave his Irish home and found a monastery on the island of Iona in 563. From there he made long journeys into the Highlands, converting the savage Picts to Christianity. On one of these journeys, as he was going to cross Loch Ness a monster appeared and seemed about to attack a monk who was swimming across ahead of the saint. Columba spoke to the monster and it turned away without harming them. We are told all this in a life of Columba written in the next century by another Abbot of Iona. It is an important document in the history of Scottish place names as it provides the first recording of many of

them, including Loch Ness. Ness is also the name
of the river that flows from the loch. It may mean
"rushing", but that is not certain. Inverness means
"mouth of the Ness". The story about Columba
does not help us with the meaning of the name, but
it is interesting to see that this name was there in the
sixth century and that even then there were tales of
a monster in the loch.

The Gaelic language spread rapidly over the
Highlands and most of the names in the northern
half of Scotland belong to it, while the Lowlands
have a mixture of Gaelic, British and English. There
must be Pictish names in both regions too but the
only Pictish word that can be definitely identified in
them is *Pit-* which seems to have meant a farm or
village. This is the beginning of several well-known
names, the second part being generally a Gaelic
addition. Pittenweem is the Pictish village near
caves; Pitlochry the same among stones.

A good many Gaelic words, such as *glen* and *loch*
are well known in England; some that are less
familiar—though common in the place names of
Scotland and Ireland—appear on pages 172–73.
One of the most important is *dun*, meaning a fort.
As in all the Celtic languages, the principal noun
comes first and description after. The many towns
beginning with this word are easy to see on a map
of Scotland. (In a few cases the "n" has changed to
"m" but the origin is the same.) Dumbarton
(earlier *Dun Breattan*) was the fort of the Britons;
Dunkeld, the fort of the Caledonians, an early tribe

mentioned by a Roman writer; Dunbar, fort on a hill-top; Dumfries, fort by a little wood; Dunoon, fort by the water.

There was so much fighting that every chieftain had his castle, and often it was known by his name. The second parts of the names Dundee and Dunfermline are probably names of early chiefs, but nothing at all is known of them. Dunblane takes its name from a holy man, St Blane, who started a monastery there.

The spreading of Christianity played a large part in naming the land. In Gaelic a church or holy place is signified by the beginning *Kil-*, which is even more common in Ireland. Kilmarnock, for instance, is the church of Ernoc, whom people called affectionately *Mo Ernoc*, which is like saying "My darling Ernoc". There were many saints of this name (some say twenty); this one was probably a relation of Columba who went with him among the Picts.

In the Lowlands where a northern form of English was the common language a church was called a kirk. Kirkcudbright (pronounced Kirkoo'-bry) is the church of St Cuthbert (note the Gaelic word-order although the words are English). Cuthbert was a shepherd boy who became a monk at Melrose, and later a bishop in Northumbria, and died on the lonely Farne Island. In his youth he travelled all over what is now the Border country, beloved by all who knew him, including birds and animals, for he had a special gift with wild creatures. He is really an English saint, but his name has no such prominence in England as it does in Scotland where it names a whole county.

There are many English names in Scotland but far more are Celtic (whether Brittonic or Gaelic) and most of them are descriptions of the land. Glasgow means green hollow; Linlithgow, lake in a damp hollow; Dalkeith, meadow by a wood; Douglas (both here and in the Isle of Man), black stream; Melrose, bare moorland; Kilcreggan, church by a little rock; Oban, little bay; Perth, a thicket; Crieff, a tree (it must have been a very special one). An odd one is Banff which means "little pig". In Gaelic folklore it was a sort of nickname for Ireland. But in Scotland was there a real little pig, or a strange Irish fancy? We can't tell. Stirling and Forfar provide two more mysteries.

In the ninth century came the Northmen raiding the coasts and adding names from yet another language. They called the deep inlets and river-mouths *fiords* as they did in Norway; in Scotland this word became "firth" and wherever you see it you can be sure that Viking ships were there. They called a narrower inlet a *vik* which we write as "wick" (but it is quite different from the common ending *-wick* in England, described on page 25). The port of Wick in the north of Scotland is a Northman's *vik*, and Lerwick in Shetland a muddy one.

It is an odd fact that the northernmost county of Britain is called Sutherland, the "south land". Only the Vikings could have called it so. They had colonies in Orkney and Shetland, in the Hebrides and on the Isle of Man, and as they sailed in their open boats among the outposts of their watery kingdoms the mainland lay often to the south. An important landmark for them was the north-west corner of Scotland which they called *Hvarf*, "the turning place". English speakers of later times, seeing the wild seas around it, have made the Vikings' "corner" into the more dramatic Cape Wrath.

Most of the names on the northern Scottish coasts are of Norse origin, and so too are those of the harbours and headlands on the Islands. But the names of the whole islands have remained much as they were when those ancient Greek sailors reached them more than a thousand years before the Vikings.

Is it any wonder that Scottish names are hard to explain, coming as they do from the speech of Picts, Britons, Scots, English and Vikings? And that was not the end, for, although the Normans did not conquer Scotland, they did have influence on its royal court and brought in a few French names, such as Beauly (*beau lieu*, "beautiful place"), where they built a monastery. But of all these six languages the one that has named the most is the Gaelic of the Scots.

13

Ireland

FROM AS far back as records go, Ireland was inhabited by a Celtic race called the Gaedels or Gaels. They had migrated there from the western coasts of Europe while a different branch of the Celts were crossing the Channel into Britain. Thus the Gaels and Britons were related, and their languages closely linked, though different in many details.

Britain, being close to Europe, had always new waves of invaders coming in, among them the Romans who for a time made it part of the civilized world. Ireland, in contrast, remained aloof and alone, untouched for hundreds of years by the outer world. Greek sailors had noted its existence and its name—written as *Ierne* or *Ivernia*—long before the birth of Christ, but neither the Romans nor the

Anglo-Saxons made any attempt to conquer this remote land.

It was in this legendary period when the Irish had their island to themselves that most of their best-known place names were formed. Like the Britons before the coming of the Romans they did not use writing, preferring to keep their folklore in their memories. Their bards, reciting long, poetic tales, were held in high honour, and a wealth of ancient legends was passed on in this way to each generation.

These legends tell of the exploits of the leading tribes, the Uliad, the Mumu and the Laigin. Centuries later, when the Vikings were making settlements on the coasts they added their own word *staeth* (meaning a place, and soon shortened to *-ster*) to these tribal names, thereby making Ulster, Munster and Leinster to signify the territories of these people. Another tribe whose legends take us back to about the time of the birth of Christ was the Connachta, whose land is Connaught.

The name of the whole island also began as a tribal name. In many spellings ranging from *Ierne* to *Eire*, it was the land of the *Eireann*, one of several names by which the Irish called themselves. Again the Vikings added another word to it, *-land* in this case, to make the familiar form by which it has been known for about a thousand years. The Irish still resent this ending and in their own language call their country *Eire*. But if you are speaking English it is reasonable to say Ireland.

One of the pleasures of the Irish in the days when the Roman rule of Britain was beginning to break down was making raids on the British coast. One object was to carry off prisoners to be used as slaves, and on a lucky day for Ireland early in the fifth century, they captured the boy Patrick, a Christian Briton. After a time he escaped, but returned again as a man to convert his captors.

The coming of Christianity was of tremendous importance to the Irish who, like all the Celtic people, were intensely religious by nature. They had worshipped many gods and goddesses, connected with the world of nature, chiefly with rivers and with old trees such as oaks and yews. Now they were fired with the love of Christ and their noblest families led the way, many of their members giving up all luxury to become monks, nuns, and hermits. Before long Ireland was known as the land of saints.

All this is reflected in Irish place names. One of their commonest first syllables is *Kil-*, and this nearly always signifies a holy place or a church. It comes from the Latin *cella*, "a cell", for the link with the Christian church brought some knowledge of Latin, as well as the art of writing. The word was first used for a hermit's cell or small monastery. The buildings of such a place were very primitive, huts made of branches daubed with mud with a little thatched church as their centre, but a fine stone cross might be set up and splendidly carved, and the fame of the holy place spread far around.

Kildare means "church of the oak-tree". Here St

Brigit founded a nunnery in the fifth century. The fact that it does not bear her name suggests that the oak was of great importance; perhaps as a centre of heathen worship which she now sanctified to Christian use, for that was the practice of the Church. There are many places called Kilbride, where churches were dedicated to her, but Kildare was her own foundation.

There are also many Kilpatricks, the best known one being in Scotland, for as regards the Church there were no divisions between the Celtic lands. Their holy men were great travellers, always out in their boats among the islands and rocky shores. Kilkenny is the Church of St Kenneth (*Cainnech* in Gaelic). He is said to have founded a monastery there and also to have gone with St Columba on one of his missions to the Picts. Kilcolumb honours St Columba himself; see page 97.

Kilmore, a name which occurs in many places, means "the big church". Killarney is "the church among sloe trees".

From the sixth century when Columba left Ireland to found his monastery on Iona, "isle of yew trees", the Irish continued to overflow into Scotland, spreading the Christian faith and with it their own language. So the Gaelic of Scotland and the Gaelic of Ireland (which may also be called Irish or Erse) are basically the same. So too the Manx language which is also Gaelic in character. In all these lands we find the same words making the place names, and as they are all mountainous there are many different words for hills and rocks. A list of the commonest will be found on pages 172-73.

Here are some Irish names describing the natural scene. Mayo (*magh eo*) is a clearing among yew trees. The first element is generally translated "plain", but that makes it sound too big; it was only a flat open space. We see it again in Armagh, "the high plain". This is a very old name as we can tell because the adjective comes first, an arrangement that is only found in the oldest kind of Gaelic. Carrick means simply a rock, a name that is found in many places; Bray, a hillside (this is the same as the Scottish *Brae-*); Bantry, mountains by the shore; Belfast, crossing-place by a sandbank; Glendaloch, valley with two lakes.

Although the people of Ireland were for many centuries all of one race they were never united. There was always fighting between the tribes and each had its strong places of defence. One of the finest of these is Cashel on its rocky hill in Munster. This name takes us back to those raids on the coast of Britain when the Romans built forts to keep the raiders off. Their word for a small fort was *castellum*. The Britons adopted this as *Castell* (as you may often see in Welsh names), and the Irish raiders picked it up as Cashel (or *Caiseal* as it is written in Gaelic).

But this was a borrowed word, of which there were few at that time. The proper Gaelic word for a fort or castle was *dun*. Dundrum means the fort on the ridge. Dun Laoghaire (pronounced Dunleary) preserves the name of a king who allowed Patrick to preach to his court. Another *dun* that might not be recognised is Donegal, "the fort of the strangers".

A smaller fort was a *rath* and this was often the dwelling-place of a chieftain. But though a great many small places begin with *Rath-*, few of them grew into big towns.

The Irish word for a simple farm, corresponding most nearly to the English *-ton*, is *baile*. This has produced the hundreds of village names that start with *Bally-* or *Bal-*. One of them that has grown famous overseas is Baltimore in County Cork, after which the American city was named. In Gaelic it is *Baile an tigh more*, "the farm near the big house".

Another *baile* that the Irish have made much of in recent times is *Baile Atha Cliath*, (pronounced Bally a Clea). It means "the village by the hurdled ford", and appears first in one of Ireland's oldest poems. This tells how the men of Ulster were stealing cattle from Leinster and fixed hurdles in the shallow river to help drive the animals across. Then the Leinster men caught up with them and a fight followed in which great deeds were done. This was near the harbour which was known as the *dubh linne*, or "black pool", another old Gaelic name. Much later when the Northmen began raiding the Irish coast they made their headquarters in this harbour, using the name they found, and the city that grew there has been known as Dublin ever since. Modern speakers of Gaelic like to use the other old name, but to the rest of the world this famous city remains Dublin.

The coming of the Vikings changed Ireland for ever. They seized the best harbours and their settlements there grew into towns. Up to that time the Irish had hardly created towns at all. They had shown no interest in trade, and did not even use money until they learnt about it from the Northmen.

As they had done in Dublin, so in many other places the Vikings carried on old names. Tipperary (the well on the River Ara), Drogheda (the bridge by the ford), Limerick (the bare land) and Cork (the swamp) were all great centres of Norse activity, but their names are purely Gaelic in origin. But in some of the Viking settlements new names of their own sprang up. Waterford, Wexford, Longford, and Carlingford all end with the typical Norse *fjord*, disguised as an English "ford". Wexford means Vikings' fiord. Carlingford was the old woman's fiord— but no one can say who she was. Wicklow is the Vikings' meadow. The name must have been given first to land near the shore, and then spread to the hills behind.

After the Vikings the next invaders were from England. In 1171 came an army led by Norman barons to which the Irish, having no unity among themselves, could offer little resistance. This was the beginning of English influence over Ireland.

From that time onwards English gradually became the language first of the ruling classes and then of almost everyone; a sprinkling of English place names came over the land; and the old names suffered from mis-spelling by those who did not understand them and a tendency to make them look English. For instance the *dun*, or fortified town where St Patrick is thought to be buried, was written Downpatrick, as if it was an English hill.

Then there were English additions to old Irish names, as at Londonderry. Here in Derry, which means "oak-wood", a colony of English settlers was planted in 1609. Because this settlement was organized by the merchant guilds of London it became known as Londonderry to distinguish it from other places of the same name, but to many Irishmen it is still only Derry.

By the beginning of this century the Irish language was nearly extinct, but since then a great effort has been made to revive it. There has also been a strong movement to reject English names and spelling and to bring back pure Gaelic forms wherever they are known. Unfortunately by the time of the revival the only surviving speakers of true Irish were uneducated, and there was no correct written form. So the enthusiasts restored the spelling of the Middle Ages when Ireland had had its own literature. This has made the names look much more difficult than they really are.

One name whose old Irish spelling has been revived, and which is well known because it is an airport, is Cobh (pronounced Cove). It is in fact a "cove" in origin, a small bay, and was so called by the Vikings whose language was very like English and often used the same words. The place was not very important until the last century when the

English government built a new harbour there and named it Queenstown in honour of Victoria. When Ireland became independant this name was rejected and Cove restored; but in Irish the sound of "v" is written "bh" (or "mh") and this is something that travellers to Cobh have had to learn.

In most cases, however, all except speakers of Gaelic continue to use the names in their long-established familiar forms, as I myself have done in this chapter.

Complications

As we have seen, the place names of the British
Isles are a mixture of many voices from long ago.
Even in England, where most of them belong to the
English language, there are still many left over from
the older Brittonic tongue, many others that are
Danish and a smaller number of French and Latin.
If we think of the whole of Britain, then the Welsh
names would swell the British numbers, while the
Gaelic in Scotland would add one more language to
make six in all—seven if you count Pictish.

So although most of the names are simple
descriptions of the landscape they come in many
different forms, and this variety is excellent, for the
more that names are different from each other the
better. Wendover means "the white stream" or "the
shining stream" in Brittonic; Sherborne and Whit-
burn come from two ways of saying the same thing

in Old English. Or if we think of dark streams, we have Blackburn in English, Douglas in Gaelic, and Dulas in Welsh, while Dawlish in Devon comes from the English pronunciation of the same word.

Penzance means "holy headland" in Cornish (there used to be a ruined church on the headland). Holyhead has exactly the same meaning. Dublin means the same as Blackpool. Pembroke means "Land's End", and so does Pentire (another way of saying it in Welsh) and also Kintyre (in Gaelic). What a good thing it is to have all these languages.

A great many of our familiar English names have been formed out of two or more languages. Luton, Taunton, Ilford, Dartford and dozens more consist of a Brittonic river name with an English word added. Lincoln is Brittonic and Latin. The first part is the same as the Welsh *llyn*, and probably referred to a deep pool in the river which may have been bigger two thousand years ago. The Romans established a "colony" of old soldiers there and called it *Lindum colonia*. All the English did was to compress it into a single word. Stratford-on-Avon comes from Latin (*strata*), English (ford) and Brittonic (Avon); Ashby de la Zouche is English, Danish and French. And so we could go on indefinitely.

The mixture varies from one region to another. The most purely English part of England is the centre of the southern half, from round about Oxford down to the Sussex coast; the most mixed is probably the north-west where Britons, Angles and

Norsemen merged together. Penrith for instance is straight Welsh, "hill ford". Ullswater belonged to a Norseman called Ulf (the wolf). Cumberland means the land of the Cymri, which is what the Welsh call themselves, but Westmoreland is as English as it sounds. Cumbria is a fitting name for all this region where the Cymri held out for a long time against the English.

All this confusion adds to the difficulty of finding the true origins of names, but also adds greatly to their interest. The Norman clerks who wrote the official documents for a long period often made things harder still by spelling names according to their own ideas. Carlisle is an example of this. In the Roman period it was *Luguvallum*, which was probably formed from the name of a local chieftain or perhaps of a God who was honoured there. (The Celtic god of light was called Lug.) By the seventh century the town name had been contracted to *Luel*. The Welsh called it *Caer Luel*, that is Castle Luel. The Normans, when they came, heard this as one word which must have sounded like "Carlile", and thought (quite wrongly) that the name ended with their French word for an island. So they wrote it as Carl*isle*. If its early history was not so well recorded, that "s" might put us on the wrong track now.

Once the original meaning of a name was forgotten, it could easily be mistaken for a different word. The Lizard Point in Cornwall was not so called because it is shaped like a lizard. The name comes from the Cornish words *lis ard* (the high court, or dwelling of a chieftain).

Apart from errors of this sort, many regular sound-changes have taken place in English and are another cause of confusion. In Chapter II we noticed the change from Old English "a" to Modern "o", and that often gives a misleading result. Gateshead, for instance, is nothing to do with a gate. It was a "goat's head", possibly fixed up on a tree or a pole in a spot where a goat had been sacrificed in a heathen ritual.

We have noticed some pairs of different names with the same meanings. In reverse, there are pairs that are now the same but have totally different origins. Sheffield in Yorkshire was "open land by the river Sheaf", but another Sheffield in Sussex was "sheep pasture".

The moral of all this is that you should never jump to conclusions about place names. The only way to be sure of the origin of a name is to find out how it appeared at the earliest possible date. England is lucky in having many splendid records from the seventh century onwards; the Celtic lands are not so well off, but each of them has some early writings. Then there are the even older records of Greece and Rome which give some accounts of these islands. But this sort of thing is not easy for you to study at first hand for yourself. Most of us must be content to accept the findings of the scholars who have worked laboriously on the subject, and look up the meanings they give in modern books (page 177). And even they are often in doubt.

However none of these difficulties should discourage you from taking an intelligent interest in the names you see around you and trying to see their origins as far as you can. If you are familiar with the commonest elements (that is, the separate parts of the names) you will be able to understand a great many; and, although there are plenty of possible pitfalls, yet a very large number of names are in fact what they appear to be. (A list of common elements may be found on pages 170–73.)

Most of the names in Britain consist of one, two or three elements, but mostly of two. In English the last one is the common noun giving the general meaning, *-ton*, *-bury*, *-minster* and so on. This is the easiest part to recognize. The other may be a descriptive word, the name of a person, or an ancient river name or almost anything, and is much more difficult to be sure of. In the Celtic languages it is the other way round; in their names it is generally (not quite always) the first part, *Pen-*, *Aber-*, *Dun-*, and so forth, that gives the main feature of the place.

Even if you can only understand half a name it is much better than having no idea of what it can be. As you drive about the country you can think, "Here was a fort", or "This was a Danish encampment", or "This was a forest clearing". You can often know where to look for the oldest part of a town by its name, because that may tell you whether people first settled down by the river or on higher ground. All sorts of events may have happened in the town later on, but the name takes you back to the first thing that made it worth talking of.

Sometimes the words are quite plain and mean what they say but still leave us wondering. One such is Maidstone. It was the maidens' stone—not just one girl. But what did they do there? We don't know. Again Morpeth means the "murder path". We should like to know more about that too. And yet these names, though we can't get very far with them, do take us back to ancient mysteries connected with those spots.

In the younger countries overseas it is not the same. When we widen our view to look at the large territories named chiefly by people from Britain we will see a very different style of name-giving. The discovery of America was one of the most exciting things that ever happened to mankind. Up to that time Europeans had no idea that that vast landmass existed. Suddenly they had a whole new world to explore, and after that more lands in the southern hemisphere.

In giving names in these new lands explorers and colonists were filled with new ideas for names, as we shall see. They had many styles of name-giving, some of them highly original. They also imported old names from their homelands, a thing that the Anglo-Saxons seem never to have done (but the Normans did it occasionally). So in North America, and other countries even farther off, the well-worn

116

old names of Britain have started new careers. But they don't tell the same truths there that they do at home. In England the name Stratford informs us that a Roman road crossed a river at that point. In Canada it only tells us that the first settlers in that place loved England and admired Shakespeare. For the ancient roots of such names the people of the younger countries must look back to Britain.

We have seen that the English have always been ready to keep old names given by earlier inhabitants if they happened to hear them, and this has happened overseas as well as in Britain. But however much explorers and colonists have made up new names, reproduced old ones from home, and adopted those of other people, there have still been some names that grew of themselves out of natural description as they have grown in England: Cape Town, Little Rock, Anchorage, Rocky Mountains, Great Barrier Reef, Bay of Islands, the Bluff. You might say some of these are not names at all, just words, but that is what names are made of and always have been. The only difference is that in Britain they are so old and often worn down by time that it may take an expert in old languages to recognize them.

Great Explorers as Name-Givers

AT THE end of the fifteenth century Europe seemed suddenly to burst open sending out exploring ships in all directions. Just as we have exploded into outer space, so men of that time passed barriers that had seemed impassable, but unlike us they discovered huge territories of which nothing had ever been known before. The new lands needed names and the first name-givers were the sea-captains who made the dangerous voyages.

One of the first in a line of great explorers by sea was Bartholomew Díaz of Portugal who in 1488 sailed far down the west coast of Africa and came at last to the end of that great continent which had seemed as if it would bar the way to the east for ever. Because fierce gales were tossing his small ship he called the southernmost point of land *Cabo*

Tormentoso, or Cape of Storms, but on his return the king of Portugal, rejoicing that the way was now open to the Spice Islands of the East, renamed it *Boa Esperanca*. This was a fine name and the other countries of Europe have all translated it into their own words. To us it has always been the Cape of Good Hope, and from it Cape Town and Cape Province have taken their names.

Soon afterwards another Portuguese sea captain, Vasco da Gama, rounded the Cape. He named a stretch of coast that he found just beyond the Cape *Natale* (or Natal). This is the Portuguese word for Christmas, for it was on Christmas Day that he first saw it. This method of naming places from the dates of their discovery, especially if they were festivals of the Church, has been used by many explorers, giving such names as Easter Island, Ascension Island and Christmas Island.

Meanwhile Columbus was seeking a way to India by sailing westward, and in 1492 he found himself among the islands of the New World, where the gentle and friendly inhabitants received him happily. Of course they had their own names for all their islands but Columbus had no idea of using those. He gave a new name to each island that he saw, and gave it with pomp and ceremony, with banners and processions and the chanting of hymns. He felt like a missionary baptizing these islands and never doubted that their new names would be a blessing to them.

Some of his names were compliments to the

royalties of Spain, but far more of them were religious. Trinidad is the Spanish word for Trinity; Dominica means Sunday, the day of that discovery. Most of his names were very long-winded, but soon shortened by those who had to use them. For instance, he called one island *Santa Maria la Antigua da Sevilla*, which means "Old St Mary's Church of Seville". This became Antigua which is simply "old". Not the meaning you would choose perhaps, but there it is.

Naturally he called one island after his own name-saint, St Christopher, but the English colonists who settled there later reduced that to St Kitts. Not all his names have lasted. He named Jamaica *Sant'Iago*, but in this case the native name first spelt *Xmayca*, "the land of springs", has survived in spite of him.

But the most important name for which Columbus is responsible, the name of the whole island group, was due to his great mistake in thinking he had reached the islands near India. This error was soon realized by other seamen and map-makers, though never admitted by him, but in spite of that we still call his islands the West Indies and their people West Indians after five hundred years. And from that first mistake another even worse one followed, the calling of all the native peoples of North and South America Indians. This is a source of confusion that can never be overcome.

While Columbus was still exploring the West Indies, an English ship commanded by the Italian-born John Cabot was nosing around the rocky coastline far to the north. But Cabot never returned from his second voyage, and though some accounts of his discoveries were given by others we know of no name given by him that still remains. But his voyages set sailors and merchants talking eagerly of the new-found land, and the splendid name, New-foundland, grew as naturally at this time as names in Britain had always done. It was being used by 1500 (before it was known that the "land" was in fact an island), the first English name to take root overseas.

In 1534 another great explorer, Jacques Cartier of Brittany, came to those North Atlantic shores, and finding an opening north of Newfoundland sailed into the mouth of the great river that leads into Canada. All along the shores of the gulf he gave names, some of which have gone while others have stayed and grown famous. Like other explorers of his time he was looking for a way to China and India—he could not know that the continent was three thousand miles wide at this point. So he sailed on cheerfully. One day when the wind was against him he sheltered in a little bay and because it was St Lawrence's day he named it after the saint. He did not know he was naming a great river, for the water was salt and he still thought it might open out into another ocean. But this name was destined to grow. Later seamen who came that way began to use it for that part of the gulf, and still it grew, until the whole great seaway was known as the St Lawrence River.

When the shores of the river had closed in on him

and foaming rapids barred his way, Cartier knew he could go no further. He had come to a large Indian village where he was welcomed with a feast, for he took great pains to be friendly with all the Indians whom he met. With some of them he climbed a high hill from which he could see far ahead; but only forests and mountains lay before him. Sadly, because his quest was ended, he named the hill *Mont Royal*, in honour of the king of France, and turned homeward. A century passed before French colonists began to build a town there, and then in their speech *Mont Royal* became Montreal.

Unlike Columbus, Cartier valued native names and preserved them when he could. When his Indian friends told him of a tribal hunting-ground called Canada he wrote that in his journal and on his chart. It was the land that lay around Quebec (another Indian name). When the French built a fort at Quebec in the next century they called the surrounding country Canada; and long afterwards when English colonists settled higher up the river they called their part Upper Canada. So the name kept on spreading until it was stretched to include a whole great country. The original meaning is not known for certain, but, whatever it was, its significance is much greater now.

What of the English explorers of that century? Of Ralegh something will be said later. Drake, who sailed round the world, has left no lasting name of his own invention. And yet he gave some. His boldest venture was when he sailed to the western

Map 2. Canada: Seamen and Explorers in the 16th and 17th centuries

side of America which only the Spaniards had reached before, and farther up the coast than they had been. There he landed and took possession of the land in the name of Queen Elizabeth, naming it New Albion. He had this name engraved on a brass plate and set up on a strong oak post among a crowd of admiring Indians. But no one followed up his bold gesture. In time the Spaniards spread up the coast calling it all by their own name, California, which comes from an old Spanish legend. New Albion is one of those lost names that never really lived; but a few years ago Drake's brass plate was dug up in a bay near San Francisco, and that is now called Drake's Bay.

Meanwhile other English sailors were trying to find a way round the north of the great land-mass and their names are still there in the Arctic where they risked their lives among the icebergs: Frobisher Bay, discovered by Martin Frobisher in 1576, Davis Straits, where John Davis sailed in 1585, Baffin Bay charted by William Baffin in 1616. The greatest of these northern adventurers was Henry Hudson, who thought he had reached the further ocean when he sailed into the great bay that bears his name, only to be disappointed when its western side again barred the way. When he refused to turn back at the onset of winter his mutinous crew set him and his son adrift in an open boat while they sailed homeward. No wonder this great expanse of water has always been Hudson Bay. He found it and died in it.

Not all explorers have their names preserved in the places they discovered. It has always been largely a matter of chance which of them have received this kind of honour. More than two and a half centuries passed after the death of Columbus before his name began to appear on the map. Long before that the New World to which he had led the way had received the name of one of those who had followed him, the Spaniard, Amerigo Vespucci, who had explored down the coast of South America, but did not merit this remarkable honour. The name "America", formed from his first name, was suggested by a German professor who had read Amerigo's account of his voyage, and it was taken up by others, chiefly because a name was badly needed. In later times some Americans wished that the United States could have been called Columbia, so that they could have a name that was all their own. But by then it was too late.

More Explorers

In the last chapter we thought of some of the early explorers of several nationalities who have contributed important place names to the English-speaking countries. Another great sea-going race were the Dutch. They followed the Portuguese to Africa, India and the spice islands beyond, and their seamen, seeking still further for lands to trade with, were the first Europeans to sight any part of Australia.

They saw only its barren northern and western coasts which they did not much like the look of, but they left a few names, such as Dirk Hartog's Island, named for a skipper who landed there in 1616, and on their maps, along the great stretch of land that they had only touched on here and there, they boldly wrote New Holland.

The greatest of all the Dutch explorers was Abel Tasman. In 1642 he set out to see how far this strange bare land extended southwards, for many thought that it reached to the South Pole. Having passed its south-western corner, he sailed on eastwards through unknown seas until he came to the land that now bears his name, Tasmania, but he did not explore it much, or even realize it was an island. He named it Van Diemen's Land after the Governor of the Dutch East Indies who had sent him on this quest. Then on he sailed again for another thousand miles until land once more barred his way, this time with high mountains rising from the sea. He named this Statenland in honour of the Dutch States-General (or parliament) but when after many months he came back to Holland the authorities there preferred to call it New Zealand to match New Holland, Zealand and Holland being the two provinces of their country.

So a whole country, and the nation that was to grow there, was named by men who had never been near it, and cared so little for it that they never sent another ship to find out more about it. And even Tasman who had indeed discovered it had not put a foot ashore. When he lowered his boats the Maoris had come out in canoes and attacked fiercely, killing some of his crew, and he drew back and sailed on without any further attempt to land. He marked the place on his chart as Murderers Bay, but white settlers of later times prefer to call it Golden Bay from its glorious stretch of sands.

Tasman sailed up the coast at a safe distance giving a few more names but only one of them has remained, Cape Maria van Diemen, named for the wife of the Governor to whom he had already done his duty. This Dutch lady is alone in strange company for her cape is close to the spot where traditionally the spirits of all the Maori dead leap into the sea to join their ancestors.

Only a few of the names that Tasman chose himself have lasted, but from his great voyage came Tasmania (changed from Van Diemen's Land in 1855), the Tasman Sea, and New Zealand, a name that has stuck in spite of the lack of any real connection with the Dutch province. The Australians rejected New Holland as the Spaniards had New Albion, but New Zealand remains as a link with the Dutchman who sailed so far, more than three hundred years ago, but failed to get ashore.

Of all the great explorers by sea no one gave so many names as Captain Cook. He contributed more to our knowledge of the globe than any other man, charting thousands of miles of coasts that were hitherto unknown. Between the year 1768, when he was first sent into the Pacific, and 1779, when he was killed by natives on a Hawaiian beach, he mapped the whole coast of New Zealand, the east coast of Australia, the west coasts of Canada and Alaska, and more islands than anyone would care to count.

With so many names to find for the capes, bays, peaks and islands that he saw from the sea, Cook knew he must ring the changes, and he used the incidents of shipboard life to supply ideas. So the coast of New Zealand still echoes with the hazards and enjoyments of his most famous voyage. At Poverty Bay he got nothing that he wanted from the Maoris, but in the Bay of Plenty they were friendly and traded food. At Cape Kidnappers some of them tried to carry off one of the crew, and at Cape Runaway some threatening Maoris were put to flight. At Mercury Bay he observed the transit of Mercury (being a skilled astronomer); at Cape Bream his men enjoyed good fishing; and we can picture the scene as he entered Twilight Bay and Dusky Sound and sailed past Cape Foulwind.

Again you may feel his presence on the Australian coast. In Botany Bay his passenger, the famous botanist, Joseph Banks, found many new plants to excite him. On Smoky Cape they saw native fires. In Thirsty Sound they found no fresh water. Cape Tribulation and Weary Bay recall some of their troubles on the Great Barrier Reef where they were nearly wrecked.

Mixed in with these "incident" names are the titles of prominent Englishmen, particularly of naval men for whom Cook, as a junior officer, felt dutiful respect. (He was only a lieutenant at this time.) Royalties and politicians also received their due; names like Grafton and Gloucester, for instance, that seem to have been chosen as English place names were actually given because they were the titles of distinguished men. These names seem much less interesting than the ones that tell of his adventures, but have often proved easier to live with. For instance, in New Zealand, the name Hawkes Bay, given in honour of old Admiral Hawke, was extended to become a whole province; but Poverty Bay remains only a bay—no one wants to call their home-town or district Poverty or Tribulation.

When he reached the northernmost point of Australia, which he called Cape York after an elderly royal duke, Cook formally took possession for England of the whole two thousand miles he had surveyed and whatever lay behind it; and for this he had to find a name. Jacques Cartier had recorded the name of Canada without realizing its future. Cook, on the other hand, thought he was naming a whole country, and felt the solemnity of the occasion. There was no native word to help him, for in spite of many attempts he had failed in making friends with the Aborigines. So he fell back on the regular style adopted by all the exploring nations when claiming territory. The Spaniards had called their American colonies New Spain; the French had used New France in the same way; English colonists in America called part of their land New England, and another colony Nova Scotia ("New Scotland" in Latin); New Albion was still in use by the Royal Navy for the Californian coast; and a tropical island had been named New Britain by an ex-pirate, William Dampier. So Cook decided on New Wales. He wrote it in his journal, but evidently was not satisfied and added the word South. New South

Wales is not an inspired name. It has lasted and made a character of its own, but instead of growing larger as Canada did it has shrunk to only part of what Cook had in mind. After two centuries of wear its people are tending to shorten it in speech to New South, and there is something to be said for that.

Cook was a very great man, but a man of deeds rather than words. He gave some delightful names—the Friendly Isles, for instance—but his invention sometimes failed, and the more important a name seemed likely to be, the more he grew formal and correct and dull.

His own plain old English surname has been attached to the highest mountain in New Zealand and the strait between the North and South islands, the little town of Cooktown in Australia where he camped while repairing his ship, a group of Pacific islands, and a deep inlet in Alaska. Not a bad collection, but with a more melodious name he might have had more honours of this sort. Tasmania, for instance, sounds very well, but you can't do much with Cook.

It fell to another naval officer, Matthew Flinders, to complete the outline of the mysterious land which up to 1800 was known only as New Holland in the west and New South Wales in the east with an unknown gap in between. Setting out in a small ship in 1801 he eventually sailed all round the continent, proving that it was indeed one. But when at last after many harrowing adventures he got back to England, made his official report, and suggested that the land be called Australia, the Admiralty rejected his idea.

The trouble was that Australia was a simplified form of *Terra Australis*, "land of the south", a name which had been in use for centuries for the land that was thought to exist at the South Pole—the region we now call Antarctica. Cook had sailed far among the ice-floes looking for it but had failed to find it. If he had, it would have been called Australia; and he would never have given this name to a land that was nowhere near the Pole. Nor would the Admiralty. But the colonists of New South Wales heard the name and liked it. They began to use it and in a few years it seemed so right that Australia could never be anything else.

It is much harder to name large places than small ones. Names are like plants put into unknown soil. Some do better than you might have expected, and some over which you have taken great trouble dwindle away. For names, like all words, are living things and once they have taken root there may be no stopping them.

17

Royal and Loyal Names

When Sir Walter Ralegh planned the first British colony in the New World he naturally deferred its naming to the queen, Elizabeth I. They were both highly original people, and scholars too, and were not likely to produce anything dull. The name they chose between them, Virginia, was a compliment to her, for she was often called "the Virgin Queen", and also well-suited to a land that was beautiful, romantic and unknown.

That first colony was a failure. Of the settlers left there in 1584 with weapons and supplies, not one survived. But the name did, and twenty years later when another attempt was made in the reign of James I, Virginia came to life again. Its new colonists, following the same idea, named their chief town Jamestown in honour of the king.

So came the first two of the many royal names that were to be spread around the world. They were chiefly used for whole colonies or their principal towns, for they seemed too important for lesser places, and they expressed the great wave of patriotism that lasted from the reign of Elizabeth I right through the whole long period of empire-building. A great many of them are in the United States, which for over a hundred and fifty years was loyal to the English crown, before it broke away to begin a life of its own.

There is room here to mention only a few. The colony of Carolina (now the states of North and South Carolina) was named after Charles I. The form chosen is derived from the Latin name *Carolus* (Charles) with a feminine ending because the Latin word for a land, *terra*, is feminine. This colony, though planned before the Civil War, was not actually started until 1663, and its chief town, Charleston, was named for Charles I's son, Charles II. Maryland was called after Charles I's queen, Henrietta Maria. It was the king who suggested this name, and it shows that he himself liked his wife to be called Mary.

Who today thinks of New York as a royal name? But it is. It was named in honour of Charles II's brother, the Duke of York, later James II, and a very unsuccessful king. It happened in 1664 when there was war between England and Holland. Up to that time the Dutch had had a colony on the American coast, its chief town being New Amsterdam. The Duke of York, who was then in charge of the Navy, sent a force to capture it, which they did without bloodshed, and when the British officer in charge had accepted the Dutch surrender, he proclaimed the new name in honour of the prince under whose orders he acted. It was a correct choice, as formal as running up the English flag, but a very dull one. Better than New Amsterdam, because less of a mouthful, but that is about all one could say for it. And yet great cities rise above dull names and give them qualities of their own. No one thinks of New York as a dull name today.

Williamsburg in Virginia was named for William III, and so also Nassau in the Bahamas as he was a prince of Orange-Nassau. Annapolis in Maryland was coined for Anne, last of the Stuart sovereigns, when she was still a young princess, and the same name was used again in Nova Scotia when she was an old queen. The ending *-polis* is the Greek word for a city, a good choice to combine with a short name like Anne. Most of the educated men of that time knew some Latin and Greek, and very useful this proved in building up names.

Next the Georgetowns began to appear—not only in America, for there were Georges on the British throne for over a century and by the end of that time there were many more British colonies. So there are Georgetowns in all directions, including the capitals of Guyana and Gambia and three West Indian islands. The American state of Georgia was

named for George II, but most of the George-
names are for George III, who reigned for sixty
years. And the names and titles of his wife and
family were scattered round the world as well.

The War of Independence put an end to royal
naming in the United States, but its citizens never
seem to have thought of changing any of the royal
names they already had. These names were their
own now, part of their land, whatever their origins.
And at that very time Captain Cook was charting
the coast of Alaska and giving more royal names to
the icy capes and inlets which would one day become part of the United States. So the future
George IV, then a boy, has his place among other
English kings in the country that rejected them as
rulers: Prince of Wales Point in Alaska and the
nearby town of Wales are his memorial there.

In all the other parts of the rapidly growing
empire, royal names continued as prime favourites.
In Canada thousands of loyal colonists who had
flocked north from the States to make themselves
new homes in a land where they could remain
British expressed their feelings by naming their
chief town Kingston. This was not by any means a
new name. There are many Kingstons in England,
all stating the fact that the place was once part of a
king's estate. But overseas it has always meant much
more. The naming of Kingston in Jamaica was an
expression of loyalty to Charles II soon after his
restoration to the throne, and Kingston in Canada
was a strong statement of loyalty to George III at

a time when other colonists had rebelled against him.

William IV, "the sailor king" who followed George IV, reigned only a few years but his name lives in King William's Town in South Africa, while his shy, gentle wife Queen Adelaide has a fine Australian city in her honour.

Then came Queen Victoria, by far the most named-after person who ever lived, even though she has no footing in the United States. The loyal colonies vied with each other to honour her. The Australians named two states for her—Victoria and Queensland—as well as a river and a desert. Canada called two large cities after her—Victoria and Regina. It was Victoria's daughter, Princess Louise, wife of a governor-general of Canada, who suggested *regina*, the Latin word for "queen", to make a change; and she herself is remembered by Lake Louise. Victoria saw to it that her husband was suitably honoured with a whole province, Alberta. Her own name crops up wherever her adventurous subjects penetrated: the chief town of the Seychelles, the harbour of Hong Kong, a mountain in New Guinea, a great waterfall in Africa, an Arctic island; and such names were given with enthusiasm for the love for her was very real.

Every sovereign since Elizabeth I has a place on the world map, and most of their consorts too, but those of this century are mostly in the Polar regions.

When colonies were growing in all directions far

more names were needed than royalty could supply, and the next choice was for those who represented the king. In later times there was a special Minister for the Colonies, but in the eighteenth century one man, generally a nobleman, assisted the king in all overseas affairs, under the title of Secretary of State. Some of these men were notable statesmen, others only mediocre. It was largely a matter of chance which ones had great cities named after them.

One of the first colonial settlements named in this way was Halifax, Nova Scotia, founded in 1749 and named after Lord Halifax, who was largely responsible for the enterprise. He deserved to be remembered there, and it was lucky that he had a good-sounding title, for his family name was Dunk.

Another name of this sort is Sydney. The expedition to establish the first colony in Australia sailed in 1788 under the command of Captain Arthur Phillip. It was to have been at Botany Bay, but when they got there Captain Phillip found another harbour, a superb one, that was better for the purpose. So he had to name it, and felt it a great responsibility. What should we do in his place? Look at the land perhaps and try to get an idea from that. But Captain Phillip was thinking of his duty to England and his loyalty to those who had sent him out, and so after toying with "Albion" he played safe with the title of the Secretary of State. There was nothing very notable about Lord Sydney, but in that moment his name became immortal.

Afterwards Captain Phillip gave some more

original names, such as Manly for a bay where he admired the manly bearing of some Aborigines who stared at him with no sign of fear, but for more important names loyalty to England came first.

Altogether naval officers played a great part in naming the outposts of empire. Not only were they the first people to reach them, but also they were sent out later as governors. In New Zealand, as in Australia, the first governor was a naval man, a Captain Hobson. He too named the place that he thought would be his capital from the Colonial Secretary, who was then Lord John Russell. But Hobson soon realized that Russell was too far north for the capital, and chose another fine harbour. So he had to find another name. This time he thought of Lord Auckland who a few years before had been First Lord of the Admiralty, and had since become Governor-General of India. Lord Auckland had nothing whatever to do with New Zealand, but he had given Captain Hobson promotion in the past, and now the captain showed his respectful gratitude.

So two beautiful southern cities were named from politicians thousands of miles away. Others were to follow. Colonial Secretaries whose names live on in towns and cities of the southern hemisphere include the Lords Hobart, Bathurst, Glenelg, Normanby, Newcastle and Kimberley. Sir George Murray, who also held this office, had his name given to Australia's greatest river, and the naming of Perth was another compliment to him, as he was the Member of Parliament for that Scottish city.

Prime Ministers, of course, were honoured in this way too, but not with such regularity. The site of Auckland, like that of Russell, was still too far from the centre of New Zealand and the seat of government was moved again. Finally it was the old Duke of Wellington who received the honour of a capital city in his name. And at the end of the century Lord Salisbury, then Prime Minister, was awarded the same distinction in Rhodesia.

Colonists' Choice

THE VERY first Englishmen—as far as is known—
to make homes in the New World were the seamen
who fished for cod around the rocky shores of Newfoundland. They may have known its coast even
before Cabot made his first voyage in 1494; certainly they were there in large numbers soon after.
Their settlements were not permanent for when
winter approached they sailed back to England to
sell their season's catch, but during the summer
months they camped in the coves where they dried
their fish in the sun, and each man named his
summer dwelling-place after his own fancy, or
mocked his neighbours, with names that still
remain: Hearts Delight, Hearts Content, Bare

Need, Seldom-come-by (now Seldom), Witless Bay, Doting Cove, and so on.

In a more formal style somebody named St John's which is mentioned in a sailor's report to the king in 1527, making it the first recorded overseas settlement. There are few written records of Newfoundland before about 1600, but when they do begin the jocular names mentioned above are found to be already there.

On the American mainland when the first official English colony was at last established naming was taken much more seriously. As we saw in the last chapter, the first duty was to the sovereign, and after that the colonists still looked to England for more names. It was the leader in Virginia, Captain John Smith, who called the wild land to the north New England. He had many adventures there, narrowly escaping death from the Indians, and recorded some of their names for their land, but like other colonists he wanted to fill it with more friendly and familiar names. He wrote an account of what he had seen and sent it with a map to Prince Charles (later Charles I) "humbly entreating that you would please to change their Barbarous names for such English that Posterity may say Prince Charles was their Godfather". The Prince, who was sixteen years old, suggested several names, among them Plymouth for a sheltered bay. A few years later the Pilgrim Fathers sailed from the English Plymouth in the *Mayflower*, and when at last they reached America and found a refuge on the coast it was exactly the place already named Plymouth.

The Pilgrim Fathers had decided ideas about place names. They did not object to Indian names for wild features such as rivers and mountains, but their own dwelling-places must have proper, respectable, civilized names, according to their own ideas. That meant English place names. As Puritans they did not approve of glorifying particular persons such as saints or kings and they made no royal names, as the Virginians did, but they gradually filled New England with the names of towns and villages from old England.

They knew little of the origins of the names they chose. If they had known more they would not have called their chief town Boston, for the original Boston in England began as "Botolf's stone", and Botolf was an Anglo-Saxon saint. His life is very obscure, but several English churches were dedicated to him. To the Pilgrim Fathers Boston meant only the prosperous little town in Lincolnshire, with a fine church tower, a place that some of them had known and loved.

Wherever the British have settled all round the world they have often longed for the sights and sounds of home. These they could not have, but a familiar name could be had at once and this was often their choice. There can hardly be a town in Britain without a namesake overseas. The Pilgrim Fathers in America began it, but Canadians, Australians, South Africans and New Zealanders have all done it too. Not so much in recent years,

because now they have their own civilized surroundings and only the new arrivals feel homesick,
but in earlier years when the journeys were im-
mense and the new land wild and strange, then the
old names were replanted overseas in all directions.
There are at least sixteen towns outside Britain
called Cambridge, twenty Oxfords, twenty Chesters
and over thirty Richmonds.

In Canada they have done the thing thoroughly.
There you may find London on the Thames in the
county of Middlesex. This is a fine gesture but the
younger city must always be over-shadowed by the
older one. The repetition of old names in new
settings really works better when the names taken
are of small villages, little-known to the world at
large; then if they win fame in a new land it is all
their own. Calgary, for instance, a fine city of the
Canadian prairies, was named by a colonist after
his boyhood home, a tiny fishing village on the
Scottish island of Mull; it is now more than a
thousand times the size of its parent. The original
meaning was probably "calf enclosure", not un-
suitable for the centre of a cattle-raising district in
Canada—but that is not the point. The point is that
colonists love names from their homelands, and the
farther away they are, the more they love them.

The Scots have always been among the most
enterprising of colonists, and their names may be
found all over the world. Of all the groups of
pioneers who ever left Britain none have journeyed
farther than those who set out from Scotland in 1847

for the southernmost part of New Zealand. There in the antipodes they surrounded themselves with the names they loved. They wanted to call their chief town Edinburgh, but very wisely chose its Gaelic form, Dunedin (page 97), and so their descendants have a name that is unique, and the old associations too. They did the same with their biggest river, calling it Clutha, the old Celtic form of Clyde, as recorded by the Romans.

Another settlement in New Zealand, this one organized by the Church of England, was named Canterbury, not so much from the Kentish city as from the mother church, which was to be their inspiration. For their chief town their young leader, Robert Godley, chose Christchurch, in affectionate memory of his Oxford College.

Once the first hunger for familiar names was satisfied, settlers overseas have generally become more original in their name-giving. Among the early American colonists some of the more serious-minded began to make up names from virtues, such as Concord, a town in Massachusetts. The Quaker, William Penn, chose Philadelphia (from the Greek for "brotherly love") for the chief town of his colony. In several places, including one of the Bahama Islands, the name of Providence was chosen, in the hope that God's providence would watch over them. This type of naming continued all across the States, giving names like Freedom, and Friendship, but has been much less used in the other English-speaking lands.

A more popular source of inspiration for naming has been wild life. America has dozens of towns with names like Beaver City, Elkton, Eagleton and so forth, all coined in the same spirit that produced Beverley and Otterburn in England. The big city of Buffalo was actually named after an Indian chief of that name, but it comes to the same result. Canada is very rich in these animal names: Red Deer, Caribou Mountains, Great Bear Lake, Beaverlodge and many more. Australia has the Swan River (originally the Black Swan River, named by an early Dutch explorer who was amazed to see black swans) and Kangaroo Island (named by Flinders on his voyage of discovery), but generally speaking, both here and in New Zealand, more formal names were preferred for towns.

Then there are names from incidents. The American Indians often named places from events that had happened there, and sometimes the white settlers translated these Indian names into English. In this way Wounded Knee became the name of a spot where a Sioux chief had been wounded. Medicine Hat in Canada is where the ceremonial headdress of a medicine man was captured or lost in a skirmish between tribes. The colonists sometimes made this sort of name too: Kicking Horse Pass in the Rocky Mountains tells its own story. In South Africa the Blood River got its name from a terrible battle there with the Zulus, and in Australia, Lake Disappointment, dried up in the heat of the desert, is a vivid link with a thirsty explorer. Such names are more interesting than second-hand ones imported from a far-off land. Or so we think looking from a distance; the colonist on the spot has often felt differently.

What the colonist often wanted in a name was something that sounded gentle, romantic, inspiring, or merely "pretty". Many of them have made up names to suit themselves, using old-fashioned words that sounded right in place names though they would not use them in everyday speech: Avonlea, Rosedale, Pinehurst and so forth. Some have chosen poetic names like Arcadia or Aurora, or literary names like Waverley, made romantic by Sir Walter Scott and melodious-sounding too. A much-admired poem, Goldsmith's *The Deserted Village*, begins "Sweet Auburn, loveliest village of the plain", and that produced a crop of Auburns overseas—*The Times World Atlas* lists nineteen.

These are a few of the ways in which names have been made in the younger countries, but there was yet another style that became the most popular of all. This was naming towns from people. At first, as we saw in the last chapter, only the most exalted people were so honoured, mostly royalties and their ministers, but after the Americans had won their independence and named their capital, Washington, from their first president, they went on to make names from popular persons of every sort. By the nineteenth century this custom had spread round the world and colonists everywhere were naming places from anyone they admired whether far away or near at hand.

This style produced so many names that it needs a chapter to itself.

19

People and Places

IT IS curious to see how the names of men and of places are sometimes woven together, back and forth, from one to the other. Think, for instance, of Washington. First there was a man named Wassa (or something like it), one of the uncivilized Angles who invaded Britain in about the fifth or sixth century. The place where he settled became known as the farm or *tun* of the Wassings, or Wassa's folk, and so Washington. Long afterwards a family who lived in that village began to use its name as a personal surname, and many centuries later again one of them migrated to America, where his grandson became the first president. Then America's new capital city was named in his honour, Washington. So it had gone from a man to a place, from a place

149

to a family, and from one of that family to a place again (a very different one), the whole process taking over a thousand years.

At least a quarter of all English surnames consist, like Washington, of the names of the villages the families once came from, and a great many overseas towns that seem to be named after English places are really named after men. This has worked out well because colonists have always liked English place names and this was one way of getting them.

This applies even more to the titles of noblemen which are nearly always place names. The habit which grew up in the new young countries overseas of naming towns from British politicians who never came within thousands of miles of them may seem to us rather tiresome. But the leading politicians, up to the present century, were generally lords, and their titles provided just the sort of names the colonists liked best. Melbourne, for instance, was named after the Prime Minister, whose title came from the Derbyshire village of Melbourne, "the mill stream". A suggestion was made that the new town should be called after its founder, John Batman, but the Prime Minister's title gave it importance, and everyone liked the sound of Melbourne.

Or again, think of Kimberley in South Africa. A child was found playing with a bright stone which proved to be a diamond, and this resulted in a rush of people to the place. For a time it was called the New Rush; that was its natural name; but as the town grew its people felt they should have "a proper name". The Minister for the Colonies was then Lord Kimberley. To the people on the spot he himself was not of much interest. But—Kimberley? Yes, they liked that. So Kimberley it became, and a pleasant-sounding name it is. Its meaning is given on page 52.

Once a place name is attached to a person—whether as surname or title—strange things can happen to it. After Wellington, the name of a small market-town in Somerset, became the title of the Iron Duke it took on a strong military character, particularly associated with knee-length boots. But of all English place names the one that has had the oddest fate is Sandwich.

First it was, exactly as it says, a village on the sands, actually a thriving little port until the sea receded from it. Later it became the title of an earldom, and when Captain Cook set out on his famous voyages it happened that the First Lord of the Admiralty, from whom he took his orders, was the Earl of Sandwich. Cook, who had a strong sense of duty, showed his respect by giving the name of Sandwich to various landmarks of the Pacific, the most important being the group of islands where he soon afterwards met his death. But the Sandwich Islands are now called by the native name of the largest island, Hawaii, and though the South Sandwich Islands in the far south and an Australian cape still bear the earl's name, it is not that that has made him famous.

The earl was not a model of good behaviour. He neglected his duties and spent most of his time gambling. So keen was he on this occupation that he often wouldn't leave the card-table to have his dinner and called instead for "a slice of beef between two slices of bread". So the "sandwich" was created. This word has gone round the world. It is as international as "O.K.", used by countless millions every day, a strange legacy from a gambling earl. The next time you say "Have a sandwich" just give a thought to the village in the sand.

Apart from titles, English surnames have an enormous variety. Whether they spring from place names or from other origins there are thousands of different ones, and this has been most useful in naming overseas towns. It is probably this diversity that made the habit of naming from people more and more popular. When other ideas failed there was always some man connected with the place who had a name that had not been used before, or not in that region.

On the whole when colonists were going to name a town from a person they have preferred one with an unusual or well-sounding name. This has come hard on famous men with short plain names like Cook. It was Cook who discovered Vancouver Island, and George Vancouver was then merely one of his midshipmen. Later Vancouver, who was English in spite of his Dutch name, returned in his ship to map it in more detail. Later still when a town on the mainland opposite the island grew important and its people wanted an impressive name they choose Vancouver. Cook was the greater man but Vancouver the better-sounding name.

Another fine city named from a rare surname is Durban. It was called after Sir Benjamin D'Urban, an English general who was one of the early governors of the Cape Province. His ancestors had been French Protestants who had found refuge in England long before, hence the French name. It was more of a problem to make a good place name to honour Sir Harry Smith, another governor of the Cape, but it was solved by running the two names together as Harrismith. Then the same idea was used for his popular wife, making Ladysmith. Original, but rather too formal perhaps. For places named from women Christian names seem more natural. Port Elizabeth, for instance, was named in 1820 by the first governor of the Cape after his wife. In Australia, Alice Springs, right in the heart of the central desert, was named by Sir Charles Todd after his wife, when he established a base there for a telegraph line in 1872. Australians often call it just Alice, a pleasant name.

A great many Australian towns are named from men, mostly with unusual surnames. Brisbane is from Sir Thomas Brisbane, a governor of New South Wales. His name came from a fierce Norman baron, whose nickname, "Brise-bane", meant "Break-bone". Another Australian echo from a Norman ancestor survives in Fremantle. It was named for Captain Fremantle of the Navy who proclaimed British sovereignty over Western Australia in 1829. The meaning of his name was given on page 73.

Darwin was named after the naturalist, Charles Darwin, whose voyage in the *Beagle* inspired him to write *The Origin of Species*. He never actually saw the place that bears his name, but it was given because of a personal link. On the *Beagle*'s next voyage the northern coast of Australia was surveyed and the Captain, who had many names to find, called one bay Darwin "after our old shipmate and friend". Darwin, then back in England, was still quite unknown, and when later on a town began to grow in this inlet its founders chose to call it Palmerston after the British Prime Minister. But later still when Darwin's name had become famous the inhabitants restored it to its proper place.

In New Zealand also the early settlers chose to name many of their towns from men and showed a special admiration for generals. Beginning with Wellington, they went on to call towns Picton, Havelock and Napier, all names of generals who were winning victories for England far away. The colonists even looked back into the past and named a whole province Marlborough in honour of the famous Duke of Queen Anne's reign, calling its chief town Blenheim after one of his battles. Such names have no link at all with the places to which they were given, and yet they show how those settlers so far from home felt a pride in England's history.

154

Christian names as place names here and there make a welcome change from the endless surnames and titles that were scattered round the empire. In Canada the men who looked after the remote trading-posts where Indians brought their furs to sell were generally known by their first names. Such a one was Jasper Hawes who in 1817 was keeping the store in the place now known as Jasper. Another was William MacGillivray who manned the trading-post on Lake Superior where his name lives on in Fort William.

Of all the places named by first names in this informal way in modern times the most important must surely be Johannesburg. In the excitement of a gold rush with thousands of eager prospectors pitching their tents, it was never clearly established which of several men in authority was the Johannes in question. It was probably Johannes Meyer, the Mining Commissioner, or possibly Johannes Rissik, the Government Surveyor. In any case the name grew as naturally as names had grown in the older countries long before. (*Johannesburg* is Dutch for "John's town".)

But on the whole in the nineteenth century, surnames were all-important, and hundreds of them were given to places overseas. One that has unique importance and certainly the highest position of all is Everest. The mountain was named in 1841 after Sir George Everest, Surveyor-General of India, who had just completed the first official survey of this region. How lucky it was that he had a fine-sounding name, with a suggestion of eternity about it. But that is just luck. The name actually comes from the little town of Evreux in Normandy, and was brought to England soon after the Conquest where it was changed by long use. Of course the mountain has its Tibetan name too, *Chomo Lungma*, but Everest is known around the world and seems exactly right.

A Babel of Tongues

PLACE NAMES everywhere echo the history of the land. We saw earlier how at least six languages have helped to form the familiar names of Britain. Each of the principal English-speaking lands overseas has also its own mixture springing from its own past; and in no two countries are the ingredients of the mixture quite the same.

Wherever the British have settled they have adopted some names from explorers of other nations, but often the most important inheritance has been the names of the native people, for these belong to the land more truly than any others, and give it a distinctive character. But in some countries they are much better preserved than in others.

If we begin with the United States, taking the names of the ten largest cities as a sample, we get at once a picture of those early colonial days when the Spanish, French and English were rivals for possession, with the native Redskins getting the worst of it. New York is English, Los Angeles Spanish—it was named by Franciscan monks who founded a mission to convert the Indians and called it after the church that St Francis built at Assissi, which was dedicated to *La Reina de los Angeles*, the Queen of the Angels.

The third largest city in America has an Indian name, Chicago. It means "the place of garlic", for the woods there smelt of the wild garlic that grew underfoot. Through these woods passed a trail linking the great lakes with rivers flowing southwards; hence its importance. Next comes Philadelphia, a Greek name given by an Englishman; then Detroit, pure French, though pronounced as if it was English. It lies on the passage between two lakes and means "the narrows", another vital link in early canoe routes.

The next in size are San Francisco (Spanish), Washington and Boston (both English) and Pittsburg, named after an English Prime Minister by a Scottish general, and St Louis (French again). So of the ten we have four English, two Spanish, two French, one Indian and one Greek but given by an Englishman.

Among the cities the Indian has the lowest score, but when we turn to rivers it is very different. As in Britain, where the English picked up most of the old river names from the Britons, so in America it was river names that the colonists learnt first from the

Indians. Mississippi means "big water"; Minnesota, "cloudy water"; Ohio, "fine highway", for rivers were the chief routes on which the Indians travelled. There were many different Indian languages and dialects, and so there is little repetition among Indian names, although their meanings are generally very simple. Michigan is "big water" in a different dialect, referring here to a lake. (And far to the south-west the Spaniards were saying just the same thing with their *Rio Grande*.) Just over half the States have Indian names and many of those come from rivers.

Canadian names are also a rich mixture of English, French and Indian. The Spaniards did not get so far north, but the early Portuguese explorers left a few names on the Newfoundland coast. There is, for instance, the headland they called *Cabo Razo*, the "bare" or "shaved" cape, which the English, seeing the racing tides there, turned into Cape Race.

The French, whose language is still very much alive in Canada, made many lively and imaginative names, even humorous ones, such as Lachine, now a busy suburb of Montreal. Here in 1668 the adventurous Sieur de la Salle established a base which his companions mockingly called *La Chine* because he was trying to find a route that would take him to China. Even the simplest French names seem often more attractive than the English equivalent would be. Lake Superior sounds very grand, but it only means Upper Lake, which would make a dull name.

The French had a great gift for making friends with the Indians though it was a dangerous game at which many lives were lost. Some of their missionaries spent years with Indian tribes learning their languages, and often made long journeys with Indian guides in their canoes. In this way they learned the native names, and later Canadians, English as well as French, have used them in positions of honour.

Five of the provinces have Indian names, all derived from lakes or rivers. Quebec means the narrows (like Detroit). The province is named from its chief city, which stands where the great St Lawrence is first penned in between high cliffs. Ontario is "fine lake" (the ending *io* means "good" as in Ohio). Manitoba is the "narrow water" of the great spirit, Manito. Saskatchewan is "swift river", and Yukon just "river" (in yet another language), like our Avon, but how different.

Among the cities, Ottawa is named from the river it stands on, and the river itself has the name of a fierce tribe who gave the French much trouble in the early days. Winnipeg means "muddy lake", though the water is clear now. Toronto cannot be explained for certain, it may mean "tree trunks in the water". It must be remembered that Indians moved about and, like ourselves, could inherit from other tribes old names of which they did not know the meanings. Another whose origin is not sure is Niagara, though people make up meanings for it. If a name truly belongs to a place with a strong character, that can be meaning enough. Niagara has its own meaning for all the world.

No names can give us a more vivid picture of old rivalries than those of the West Indies. In the English-speaking islands they are chiefly English, Spanish and native Indian, in that order. The natives were cruelly treated by the Spaniards and few of their names survived, but Jamaica is one (page 120) and Bahama another. (The Bahamas group is named from one of its islands.) The first to be sighted by Columbus was called by its own people *Guanahani*. He renamed it *San Salvador* (Holy Saviour) in gratitude to God. Then English buccaneers moved in and for centuries it was known as Watling Island after John Watling, "a hardened old pirate" who lived there. Now it is officially San Salvador again, and the Columbus Monument stands close to Victoria Hill. What a mixture of personalities in a small space.

Jamaica too has strangely assorted names, or so they seem to a newcomer. Where else could you find Spanish Town and Alligator Pond in Middlesex; and Reading next to Anchovy, both in Montego Bay, a Spanish name well known to Drake? Barbados is a Spanish name, "the bearded ones", alluding to the trees covered with trails of moss. Its chief town, Bridgetown, sounds very English, but it was at first called Indian Bridge, a relic of the earlier inhabitants.

There is no lack of mixture in South Africa, where the naming is chiefly shared between English and

L

Dutch (or Afrikaans), with a sprinkling of Portuguese along the coast. But the native names have little prominence. The Dutch showed no interest in them and the first English settlers seemed to prefer English names to any others. However during the nineteenth century their outlook changed. A wave of sympathy for the black races, originating in England, brought about the abolition of slavery, and an urge to know more about the native peoples. The explorations of men like Dr Livingstone opened up new territories, and in these lands, colonized by the British within the last ninety years, nearly all the place names are African. Some English names that were given in the early years have been discarded since, but Livingstone remains in Zambia and richly deserves to do so.

Of the once-British countries of Central Africa only Rhodesia retains an English name. It was coined by the editor of a local newspaper in 1890 from the surname of the pioneer, Cecil Rhodes. But apart from its capital, Salisbury, most of its place names are native. If you compare them on a map with those of the Cape Province, settled by the English in 1820, you will see how tastes and opinions have changed.

In both Australia and New Zealand the languages are less mixed than in other English-speaking lands. Each has a few—very few—Dutch and French names left by early explorers, but almost all their names come from English or the native tongues.

As far as English naming goes, their styles are

rather similar, their main themes being distant royalties, statesmen, admirals and generals, with some governors, explorers and other local personalities. The liveliest names come from the "diggers" on the "rushes" after gold and other metals. In Australia they have produced such names as Iron Knob, Silverton, Golden Ridge, Southern Cross (named by two prospectors who found their "lucky strike" by starlight), Rum Jungle and Humpty Doo.

But fortunately both these southern lands are rich in native names, and in these there is no likeness between them. In Australia they have a strong primitive rhythm which makes them unforgettable, but many have no known meaning. Murumbidgee is "big water" (like Mississippi); Yarra, just "river", Ballarat, a camp in a swamp; and Woomera, the Aborigine's throwing-stick, a kind of boomerang. But for many others such as Paramatta, and the amusing Woolloomooloo, meanings can only be guessed. It is not even known for certain what Canberra means. The important thing is that, as with Ottawa, the name chosen for the capital city was the native one that really belonged to the chosen site, a name unique in the world. This happened in 1911, when the white man's respect for the black was far greater than it had been in the first days of colonization.

The native names of New Zealand are entirely different from those of Australia. Whereas the Aborigines spoke in many languages and dialects of a primitive sort, the Maoris had one highly developed, poetical language that is still in living use. At the advance of white settlers the Aborigines had melted away, but the Maoris stood their ground, and it was only by making friends and learning their language that the new arrivals could avoid being killed and eaten. The missionaries who risked their lives by living among them learned Maori well and recorded names carefully. So the native place names of New Zealand are well understood, except for some of the oldest which have about them some of the mystery that very old names have everywhere.

Much the commonest element in Maori names is *Wai-* (pronounced Wye) which means "water"; Waikato is strong water; Waitangi, water of weeping; Wairau, many waters; Waimate (pronounced Wye-matti) dead water—a still pool. These are simple names and there are many such; others are concerned with historic events and fanciful legends. Rangitoto, the island in Auckland harbour, means "day of blood" because a legendary hero was wounded there. Wakatipu, a long narrow lake among mountains, is "the canoe of the goblin"; the biggest lake, Taupo, is in full *Taupo nui a Tia*, "the big feather-cloak of Tia". Many names are very long but there are short forms for practical use, and often there are stories that explain them. The name of the volcano Tongariro consists of the words "south wind carried". They are part of a story telling how one of the early heroes was dying of cold on the mountain top and "the south wind carried" his voice to his sisters far over the sea and they sent a magic fire to burst out of the rock and warm him. Maori place names must be among the most imaginative in the world.

We have been looking at lands where the British have both made new names of their own and have also gathered up and adopted names that were there before them, and we can see that the mixture gives a good result. There are other places, such as India, where the British were once in possession but made hardly any new names at all because the land had its own long history of civilization and was already richly named. This was very different from a great empty land like Australia, with no permanent settlements and few inhabitants—and those difficult to contact.

The only land where there were no old names to inherit is Antarctica. The names placed there in modern times are mostly those of the explorers—of several nations—who have been there, and of distant royalties. As yet they seem stiff and formal. Names need human history to make them live and no doubt these Polar ones will have more of it in time. They are young yet. Old names rich in associations with the place where they belong have something which new ones must lack for a time. That is why we should take good care of the old ones.

And Now The Moon

AND WHAT about the moon? Although it has never had any people of its own to name it, yet many of its features have names that are centuries old. As soon as the first telescope had been constructed (by the Italian, Galileo, in 1609) the astronomers of Europe began to study the details of the moon and to give them names. At that time it was thought that the darker areas were seas and they were given names like *Mare Tranquilitatis* (Sea of Tranquillity) and *Mare Imbrium* (Sea of Rains). The names were given in Latin because that was then the international language of scholars, but nowadays the scientists of the various countries concerned often translate them into their own languages. And though it is now known that the dark regions are not seas at all, yet these names are respected because of their honourable old age.

The same seventeenth-century astronomers who named the "seas" also began the practice of calling the craters after famous men of science of all times and nations. This too has worked out well because such men as Plato, Archimedes, Ptolemy and Copernicus deserve to be honoured but few of their names are found as place names on earth. The idea has been continued and as there are plenty of craters, so the names of modern scientists are joining the great names of the past.

Less successful are the names of mountain ranges reproducing those of Europe—Apennines, Carpathians and so on. The moon, so strange and different from the earth, should have names of its own, not mere copies of those on earth.

Now that men have been to the moon, more names are needed for details never seen before. Let us hope that those who give them will show imagination, originality and a sense of fitness, and that the different nations concerned will respect each other's names so that those that are chosen will last and grow in interest as centuries pass by. For place names can last as long as there are men to speak them.

Notes on Languages

Brittonic (sometimes called **British**) is the name given to the language spoken by the inhabitants of Britain up to the fifth century A.D. After that it survived as **Cornish** (which died out in the eighteenth century) and **Welsh** which is still very much alive.

Gaelic is the language of Ireland, the Scottish Highlands, and the Isle of Man. In Ireland it may also be called **Erse** or **Irish.** Scottish and Manx Gaelic (which are only just surviving) differ from it only slightly.

The Brittonic and Gaelic languages are **Celtic**. The Celts were a race who spread across Europe from about 500 B.C. and entered Britain and Ireland in these two distinct groups.

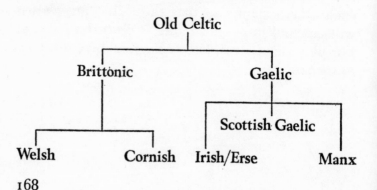

Old English (see below) is the language of the Anglo-Saxons from the time of their invasion of Britain in the fifth century up to 1100. From then to 1500 the language is called **Middle English**; since then **Modern English**.

Old Norse was the language of the Northmen (from Norway), also called Vikings, who harried the coasts of Scotland, Ireland, Man, Wales and Cumbria. The Danes who chiefly raided England were very like them and their language was almost the same. Norse and **Danish** were also closely related to English.

A GRAMMATICAL NOTE

Old English, from which most of the place names of England are formed, differed in many ways from Modern English. Many words had a variety of grammatical endings (as they do in German and Latin) that have long since gone. One that often remains in place names showed possession. We always now add *'s* to make a noun possessive. In Old English many nouns did this (actually the ending was then -*es*), but for those that ended in "a" or "e" the possessive sign was -*an*. Thus "Daga's homestead" was *Dagan ham*, now Dagenham. This explains the 'en' that occurs in the middle of many names, such as Coventry and Daventry, and the "n" in Bognor, Putney, etc.

Some Common Place Name Elements

These elements may make complete place names, but more often they are only parts.

1. English

These elements are shown as they appear in modern names. Some have become confused together and for these the Old English forms are given also. (D.) indicates Danish origin.

barrow, -beare, (O.E. *bearu*), a wood, page 42, 46

-barrow, -borough, -burgh, (O.E. *beorg*), a hill or mound, 46

borough, -burgh, brough, bury, (O.E. *burg*), a fortified place, 28–9, 31–3

-by (D.), a farm or village, 64

chester, -caster, -cester, (Lat. *castra*), a Roman town, 29–31

combe, a deep valley, 47

dale (D.), a wide valley, 65

dean, -dene, -den, a small valley, 46

-don, down, a hill, 44–5

-ey, -y, (O.E. *ea*), a river, 24, 36

-ey, -y, (O.E. *ieg*), an island, 65

-ham (O.E. *ham* with a long a), a homestead, 24, 26

-ham (O.E. *hamm*), a water meadow, 51

hithe, -eth, -ey, a landing-stage, 38

holm (D.), a flat-topped island, 65, 69
holt, a thick wood, 42
hope, -hop, -op, a small sheltered valley, 47
hough, how, hoo, hoe, -ow, -o, a rounded hill, 24
hurst, a wooded hill, 42
-ing, generally a tribal group, 50–2
leigh, -ley, a clearing in woods, 43
-low, -law, a hill or mound, 46
mere, -mer, a lake, 24
-ness (Eng. and D.), a cape, 64–5
stead, -sted, a place, 24
stoke, stow, a meeting-place, 58–9
thorpe (D.), a small village, 64
thwaite (D.), a clearing in woods, 64
-ton, enclosure, farm, village, 22–4
wick, -wich, a village or trading place, 25–6
worth, worthy, enclosure, farm, 25

2. Welsh—pages 87–93

aber, river-mouth
afon, river
bach, fach, little
bont, pont, bridge
borth, porth, port
bryn, hill
caer, fortress
castell, small fort
craig, graig, a rock
cruc, gruc, a hill
coed, goed, a wood
cwm, a valley
din, dinas, fort, town
du, ddu, black
eglwys, church
fach, as *bach* above
fawr, mawr, great
foel, moel, bare hill
fynydd, mynydd, mountain
glyn, deep valley
goed, as *coed*, above
graig, as *craig*, above
gruc, as *cruc*, above
gwyn, wyn, white

heli, salt water

lis, llys, a court

llan, church

llech, flat stone

llyn, a lake

llys, as *lis,* above

mawr, as *fawr,* above

moel, as *foel,* above

mor, the sea

mynydd, as *fynydd,* above

pen, end or headland

pont, as *bont,* above

porth, as *borth,* above

pwll, pool

rhos, ros, rough moorland

rhyn, cape

traeth, sandy beach

tre, tref, farm

wyn, as *gwyn,* above

y, yr, the, of the

ynys, island

ystrad, wide valley

Note: Cornish

The elements of Cornish names are very like the Welsh ones, but spelt in a more English style and without mutations. *Pen-* and *Porth-* are the same. *Car-, Lan-, Pol-* and *Ros-* correspond to the Welsh *Caer-, Llan-, Pwll-* and *Rhos-* (see above). The commonest Cornish element is *Tre-,* a house or farm.

3. Gaelic—pages 96–100, 104–7

(as they appear in Scottish and Irish place names as commonly spelt in English)

Ach-, Auch-, a field

-an, little

Ard-, Aird-, height

Balla-, Bal-, Bally, a farm

-beg, small

Ben, Ban-, a peak

Bri-, Brae, hillside

Carn, Cairn, stony hill

Carreg, Carrick, a rock

Cashel, a castle

Clack, a stone

Derry, oakwood

Drum-, a ridge

Dub-, Dou-, black

Dun, a fortress
Glen, narrow valley
Glas-, greeny blue
Inver-, river-mouth
Innis, Inch, island
Kil-, church or holy place
Kin-, end or head
Knock-, a small hill
Kyle, narrow water
Lis-, court or royal dwelling

Loch, Lough, lake
-more, great
Rath-, small fort
Ros-, -rose, moorland or cape
Slieve, range of hills
Strath, wide valley
Tir-, -tire, land
Tom-, a round hill

Some Useful Dates

The British Isles

From about 500 B.C. onwards	Celts from Europe (Britons and Gaels) coming into Britain and Ireland
About 330 B.C.	The Greek Pytheas sails round Britain
55 B.C.	Julius Caesar invades Britain
A.D. 1	Birth of Christ
From A.D. 43 to A.D. 410	Roman occupation of Britain Christianity reaches Britain during this period
About 432	St Patrick preaching in Ireland
From about 450 to about 650	Angles and Saxons invading Britain and spreading over it; Scots (from Ireland) spreading into "Scotland"
563	St Columba founds monastery on Iona
597	St Augustine lands in Kent
655	Death of last heathen king; all England Christian
731	Bede's *History of the English Church*
About 800	Viking raids begin
848	Scotland united under Kenneth I

174

878	King Alfred defeats Danes; establishes Danelaw
937	Danelaw reconquered; England united
990 onwards	More Danish attacks
1066	Normans conquer England
1086	Domesday Book compiled
1171	Anglo-Norman army conquers Ireland
1283	English conquest of Wales

Overseas

1488	Díaz rounds Cape of Good Hope
1492	Columbus reaches the West Indies
1494	Cabot reaches Newfoundland region
1534	Cartier in the St. Lawrence
1579	Drake in the Pacific
1584	First colony in Virginia
1603	French colony at Quebec
1620	Pilgrim Fathers sail in the *Mayflower*
1642	Tasman sights New Zealand
1650	Dutch settle at the Cape of Good Hope
1684	British capture New York from the Dutch
1700–1815	Wars with France, on and off, by sea and land
1763	All French colonies in North America ceded to Britain
1769–1779	Voyages of Captain Cook
1776	American Declaration of Independence

1783	British Loyalists from U.S.A. settle in Canada
1788	First settlement in Australia (Sydney)
1801–1803	Flinders's voyages round Australia
1814	British missionaries in New Zealand
1815	Cape of Good Hope ceded to Britain
1840	New Zealand officially British
1853–73	Livingstone in Africa
1889	Rhodesia founded
1900	Federation of Australian colonies
1909	Union of South Africa

Sources and Further Reading

There are many books for adults about the place names of England. The one that gives the most information is *The Concise Oxford Dictionary of English Place-Names* by E. Ekwall (Oxford, first published in 1928), which you will find in any good library.

When you look up a name in this book you may find the many abbreviations confusing. But a list near the beginning gives their meanings, and you will only need to know a few of them. The ones that come directly after the name show the county or counties in which it occurs. The same name may exist in several places, and the same explanation will not necessarily apply to all of them. Then the earliest known forms of the name are given, and there are abbreviations for the sources in which they are found. Some important ones that you should be able to recognize are: Ptol., Ptolemy (a Greek scholar who wrote about Britain in about A.D. 150); ASC, *Anglo-Saxon Chronicle* (an account of yearly events written in English monasteries during the whole Anglo-Saxon period); and DB, *Domesday Book* (compiled in 1086). Another abbreviation that occurs often is BCS, which refers to a collection of charters or grants of land from a very early date.

You may find that several lines are taken up with early examples of the name from different sources before you come to its meaning. Even then if it contains a common element like *tun* you may have to look that up separately.

An important series of studies of the names in each county is being published gradually by the *English Place-Name Society*, which can at present (1974) be contacted by writing c/o the School of English Studies, The University, Nottingham. Each volume is called *The Place-Names of—* (followed by the county name). They go into much more detail in each locality than the *Oxford Dictionary* mentioned above, but so far only about half the counties have been done.

A very useful book is *The Names of Towns and Cities in Britain*, by W. H. F. Nicolaisen, M. Gelling and Melville Richards (London, 1970). This deals only with towns of a certain size but has the great advantage of including towns from Wales and Scotland as well as England. It is in dictionary form, but in an easily readable style.

English Place-Names, by K. Cameron (published by Batsford, London, 1961), is a general discussion of English names by an expert.

Place-Names of Scotland, by J. B. Johnson (London, 1934), is a useful dictionary, but much work remains to be done on Scottish names.

On the whole there are very few books available on Scottish, Welsh or Irish place names, but scholars are working on them now. In the meantime all the best guide books to these countries, especially the *Blue Guides* and the *Shell Guides* give a lot of help on this subject.

The only book that gives a general picture of names all over the British Isles and overseas too, besides this one that you are now reading, is its longer and fuller version, *Place-Names of the English-Speaking World*, by C. M. Matthews (published by Weidenfeld & Nicolson, London, 1972).

A special mention must be made of the Ordnance Survey *Map of Roman Britain* (3rd edition, 1956) which lists all the known names in Roman Britain and shows their sites.

For the overseas countries the following are recommended:

Australia: *The Australian Encyclopedia* (edited by A. H. Chisholm in 10 volumes) especially Vol. 7 (Sydney, 1965)

Canada: *The Origin and Meaning of Place-Names in Canada*, by G. H. Armstrong (Toronto, 1930); and *Encyclopedia Canadiana* (Ottawa, 1956)

New Zealand: *The Story of New Zealand Place-Names* (Wellington, 1953) and *A Dictionary of Maori Place-Names* (Wellington 1963), both by A. W. Reed

South Africa: *The Encyclopedia of Southern Africa* (edited by Eric Rosenthal, London, 1961)

The United States: *American Place-Names* (a dictionary published in New York 1970) and *Names on the Land* (a very readable book—New York, 1945) both by G. R. Stewart

The chief sources for these names are accounts written by early colonists and explorers. Sea-captains, for instance, have always kept logs of their voyages, and in the journals of Columbus, Cartier and Cook, to name three of the greatest, one can read their own accounts of the names they gave and why they chose them.

In the younger countries, as also in Britain, those who want to find out more about the names in their own locality are advised to go to the nearest reference library and ask what is available on the local history. Most places have printed accounts of their own early history and these generally include whatever is known about the origin of the local names. Unfortunately books of this kind are not always to be trusted on this special subject, and their authors sometimes repeat fanciful explanations that have no foundation in truth. This is especially true of some old-fashioned guide books. But in recent years there has been much more general interest in the proper scientific study of place names, and modern books of local history are likely to be more reliable. In any case your library will help you.

Index of Place Names

Names for which no country is indicated (excepting those of some islands) are all in Britain. More details about their locality will be found in the text. When the name is a common one found in several districts the meaning given is the usual one that is true for most of them.

References to the separate parts of place names are indexed under "elements", and a list of some of the most common elements may be found on pages 171–4.

INDEX

Index of People

See also the place name index

Alfred, King, 19, 63
Anne, Queen, 135
Arthur, King, 31, 35
Augustine, St, 57

Bede, the Ven., 61
Brigit, St, 104
Brychan, King, 88, 90

Cabot, John, 120–1, 141
Cartier, Jacques, 121–2, 130
Charles I, 134, 142
Charles II, 134, 136
Columba, St, 97, 105
Columbus, Christopher, 119–20, 125, 161
Cook, James, 128–32, 136
Cuthbert, St, 99

Dampier, William, 130
Diaz, Bartholomew, 118
Drake, Francis, 122–4

Edward I, 81
Elizabeth I, 124, 133–4

Flinders, Matthew, 131, 146

Galileo, 166
Gama, Vasco da, 119
George II, 136
George III, 136
George IV, 136

George V, 83

Henry VIII, 81
Hobson, William, 139
Hudson, Henry, 124

John, King, 78
James I, 133
James II, 134
Julius Caesar, 15, 35

Oswald, King, 57, 60

Patrick, St, 104, 106, 109
Penn, William, 145
Petroc, St, 59
Phillip, Arthur, 138
Pilgrim Fathers, 142–3
Ptolemy, 94, 179
Pytheas, 15

Ralegh, Walter, 133
Rhodes, Cecil, 162

Smith, John, 142

Tasman, Abel, 127–8

Vespucci, Amerigo, 125
Victoria, Queen, 110, 137

William I, 20, 70–1, 74, 75
William III, 135
William IV, 137